GARDEN FRESH
SOUPS & SALADS

by Verna Meyer

Dillon Press, Inc.
Minneapolis, Minnesota

Table of Contents

Soups 9

    A Good Start for Good Soups 11

    Consommés 14

    Cream Soups 17

    Dinner-in-a-Bowl 21

    Hot and Hearty Favorites 27

    Potages 31

    Summer Soups 41

    Combination Soups 46

    Special Choice Soups 48

    Accompaniments to Soups 52

Salads 59

    Classic Salad Dressings 61

    Green Salads 63

    Cabbage and Spinach Salads 67

    Vegetable Salads 71

    Fruit Salads 77

    Main Course Salads 80

    Hors-d'Oeuvres 86

    Salad Ensembles 89

    Accompaniments for Salads 91

Index 94

The editors and publishers wish to thank the United Fresh Fruit and Vegetable Association for permission to use the photographs between pp. 32 and 33, and pp. 64 and 65.

SOUPS

"Beautiful soup, so rich and green,
Waiting in a hot tureen!
Who for such dainties would not stoop
Soup of the evening, beautiful soup"

Lewis Carroll,
Alice in Wonderland

GOURMET SOUPS FOR FAMILY AND FRIENDS!

Who does not welcome a bowl of hot soup on a cold day, or a chilled soup on a hot day? There is a place for soup in almost every menu, either before the main course, or as a hearty meal in itself.

Whether you start with your own homemade stock or use one of the easy soup bases on the market, it is important to remember that while the stock provides the flavor, much of the nourishment of the soup lies in what is put *into* the stock. Fresh vegetables like peas, beans, lentils, onions, carrots, beets, cabbage, and grains such as barley and rice --- these and many more can be used to improve the nutritive value of soup.

And don't throw away those coarser leaves of greens when preparing vegetables! Let the stock pot put those discarded leaves, plus the water that vegetables have been cooked in, to good use.

It is important to cook vegetables only to the point of tenderness when preparing them for soup. Never overcook! Also, vegetables should be cooked separately and added last. If a soup is to be served again the following day, cook and add a fresh supply of vegetables. When parsley is called for, always use the stems, reserving the tops for garnish. The stems provide the best flavor.

In addition to these flavorful and nutritious soup recipes, create your own, using these as basic guidelines. If you haven't discovered it already, you'll soon find that a large soup pot and soup tureen are two of the most useful items you can own.

A GOOD START FOR GOOD SOUPS

QUICK AND EASY BROTH

In a hurry? There are many excellent beef and chicken soup bases marketed commercially in the form of canned broth, bouillon, cubes, granules, and pastes. These are all fat-free and make fine stock. Follow package directions to see how to substitute them for Brown or White Stock in the following recipes. Keep in mind, however, that these broths may be more highly spiced than homemade, so season your soups accordingly.

Bottled clam juice makes an excellent fish stock for fish soups.

VEGETABLE STOCK

For a good vegetable stock, save the juice that vegetables have been cooked in, storing it in a jar in the refrigerator. Or, make a stock by boiling vegetables in water. Season to taste.

Homemade stocks are easy and fun to make if time is not a factor. Basic stock recipes are included for those who want to start from scratch!

BROWN STOCK

4 pounds beef, meat and bone	3 sprigs parsley
3 quarts water	5 whole cloves
1 onion, chopped	1 tablespoon salt
3 carrots, sliced	8 whole peppercorns
1 turnip, sliced	1 bay leaf
2 stalks celery, cut up	

Place meat and bones in roasting pan. Roast in a 400° oven until meat is well browned, about 30 to 40 minutes. Transfer to soup kettle and add remaining ingredients. Heat to boiling and skim off foam. Reduce heat and simmer 3 to 4 hours, skimming as needed. Strain through cheesecloth. Allow broth to cool and remove fat. Stock is now ready to use. Makes about 2 quarts.

WHITE STOCK

4 pounds chicken or veal, meat and bones	**1 onion, sliced**
	1 tablespoon salt
3 quarts water	**6 whole peppercorns**

Place meat and bones in roasting pan. Roast in a 400° oven until meat is lightly browned. Transfer to soup kettle and add remaining ingredients. Heat to boiling and skim off foam. Reduce heat and simmer 3 to 4 hours. Strain through cheesecloth. Allow broth to cool; remove fat. Stock is now ready to use. Makes about 2 quarts.

BOUILLON

To make bouillon, simply strain Brown or White Stock. Because it is strained, bouillon rather than stock is an appropriate choice for a light, hot drink.

CONSOMMÉ

Consommé is a clarified stock that has been refined beyond straining. To clarify stock for consommé, add 1 slightly beaten egg white for each quart of stock. Boil 2 minutes, stirring constantly. Strain stock through cheesecloth.

HAM STOCK

1 ham bone or 2 ham shanks	**1 onion, chopped**
2½ quarts water	**2 stalks celery, cut up**
1 carrot, sliced	

Place bone or shanks in soup pot. Add water and vegetables. Heat to boiling, skimming off fat if necessary. Cover and simmer about 2 hours. Remove from heat and strain stock through a fine sieve. The ham meat may be removed and added to the soup or chopped for ham salad.

Béchamel is a basic white sauce and is used in most cream soups and white sauces.

SAUCE BÉCHAMEL

1 cup milk	2 tablespoons flour
2 tablespoons butter	½ teaspoon salt
½ small onion, minced	⅛ teaspoon white pepper
	⅛ teaspoon nutmeg

Heat milk. Melt butter and sauté onion until transparent. Stir in flour. Cook and stir over low heat 2 minutes. Do not let this brown. (This is called a roux.) Remove from heat. Gradually stir in milk. Heat to boiling, stirring constantly. Strain and transfer to double boiler. Stir in salt, white pepper, and nutmeg. Cook about 5 minutes. Thin with choice of liquids.

CREAM OF CHICKEN STOCK

1 recipe Sauce Béchamel (above)
2 quarts White Stock, Chicken (p. 12)
  or chicken broth

Make Sauce Béchamel. Thin with stock or broth, adding the liquid gradually. Correct seasoning. This is basic for many cream soups. Makes 9 cups.

CONSOMMÉS

CONSOMMÉ BOUQUETIER

Carrots
Celery
Turnip
Green pepper

1 recipe White Stock, Chicken
(p. 12)
2 tablespoons dry sherry,
if desired

Prepare a garnish for the consommé by cutting the vegetables into interesting shapes and boiling in a little of the stock until fork-tender. Place vegetables and stock in which they were cooked in soup tureen. Heat the remaining stock to boiling and pour into tureen. Add sherry if desired. Makes 6 servings.

CONSOMMÉ ARGENTEUIL

1 cup fresh asparagus tips   6 cups Brown Stock (p. 11)
Seasoning to taste

Cook asparagus tips in 1-inch of boiling salted water until fork-tender, reserving cooking liquid. Bring stock to the boiling point and add seasoning. Add asparagus tips and liquid. Serve with a cheese bread. Makes 8 servings.

CONSOMMÉ BRUNOISE

2 small carrots, diced
1 small turnip, diced
1 stalk celery, diced
5 green onions with tops,
    sliced
Salt

Sugar
3 tablespoons butter
1 cup Chicken Consommé (p. 12)
2 tablespoons cooked green peas
2 tablespoons cooked green beans
5 cups Chicken Consommé (p. 12)
Snipped parsley

Place diced carrots, turnips, celery, and onions in large pot; lightly season with salt and sugar. Sauté vegetables in butter until well-coated, but not brown. Add 1 cup consommé and boil gently until vegetables are fork-tender. Just before serving, heat the remaining 5 cups of consommé. Add to sautéed vegetables. Add the peas and beans. Heat well. Pour into tureen and garnish with parsley. Makes 6 servings.

CONSOMMÉ MODERNE

1 avocado, not too ripe	4 cups Brown Stock (p. 11)
Ascorbic acid solution (2 cups water and 1 ascorbic acid tablet or lemon juice)	2 tablespoons dry sherry, if desired

Peel and pit avocado; cut into cubes or balls. Place pieces in ascorbic acid solution or sprinkle with lemon juice. Cover tightly. Heat stock. Add sherry, if desired. Drain avocado and add to stock. Serve in cups. Makes 6 servings.

CONSOMMÉ ROYALE

1 recipe Brown Stock (p. 11)   1 recipe Royale (below)

Make a good strong consommé from beef stock. Place a few cubes of Royale in cups and pour very hot consommé over them. Makes 6 to 8 servings.

ROYALE

2 eggs	*Dash white pepper*
2 egg yolks	*1 tablespoon chopped parsley, or*
½ cup Beef Consommé (p. 12)	*1 teaspoon curry powder*
Dash salt	

Beat eggs and egg yolks. Add consommé, salt, pepper, and parsley. Pour into a well-buttered 10x6x½-inch baking dish. Place in a pan of water. Bake in 325° oven 15 to 20 minutes or until knife inserted halfway to center comes clean. Cut into cubes. (If curry is used instead of parsley, this specialty is then known as Consommé Royale à la Indienne.)

ONION AND TOMATO CONSOMMÉ

3 onions, sliced	2 sprigs parsley
1 clove garlic	3 whole cloves
1 stalk celery	4 cups Brown Stock (p. 11)
1 carrot	2 cups tomato juice
Chopped basil	

Cut onion slices in half and sauté in butter until transparent. Add garlic, celery, carrot, parsley, and cloves. Stir in stock and cook 20 minutes. Strain and discard the vegetables. Add tomato juice and simmer 10 minutes. Correct seasoning and garnish with chopped basil. Serve with rounds of toast topped with grated cheese and lightly broiled. Makes 6 servings.

LEEK AND CELERIAC CONSOMMÉ

1 medium celery root (celeriac)	2 leeks
1 quart White Stock,	2 tablespoons dry sherry,
Chicken (p. 12)	if desired

Cut celery root very fine and cook in 2 cups stock until fork-tender. Cook leeks in remaining stock until tender. Strain; discard the leeks. Combine all stock. Heat before serving and add sherry if desired. Serve in cups accompanied with Curry Rolls (p. 53). Makes 4 servings.

CREAM SOUPS

CREAM OF BROCCOLI

1 bunch fresh broccoli	1 cup Sauce Béchamel (p. 13)
4 cups White Stock, Chicken	2 egg yolks
(p. 12), or Chicken broth	2 tablespoons light cream
	2 teaspoons butter

Cook broccoli in 3 cups chicken stock. Drain, reserving liquid, and blend broccoli in blender or put through a sieve. Strain reserved stock and stir in Sauce Béchamel and broccoli. Taste for seasoning. Add remaining cup of stock if soup is too thick. Just before serving, beat yolks with cream. Heat the soup. Stir small amount hot soup into egg mixture; gradually return to hot soup, stirring as you add. Cook and stir 1 minute. Serve with croutons. Makes 6 servings.

CREAM OF VEGETABLE

¼ cup carrots, diced	½ cup White Stock, Chicken
¼ cup turnips, diced	(p. 12), or chicken broth
¼ cup celery, diced	1 cup barley, cooked
¼ cup leeks, sliced	1½ quarts Cream of Chicken
1 tablespoon butter	Stock (p. 13)
	Snipped parsley

In large pot, sauté the vegetables in butter 3 minutes. Add Chicken stock. Cook until vegetables are fork-tender. Heat the Cream of Chicken Stock and add barley and cooked vegetables. Heat well. Pour into tureen and garnish with parsley. Makes 6 servings.

CREAM OF LETTUCE

2 heads lettuce
6 green onions, chopped
4 tablespoons butter
1 clove garlic
1 tablespoon parsley
1 teaspoon salt

White pepper
2 cups water
4 cups White Stock,
    Chicken (p. 12)
2 egg yolks
2 tablespoons light cream

Chopped parsley

Wash and dry lettuce and separate leaves. Sauté onion in butter and add garlic on a wooden pick. Add parsley, salt, pepper, lettuce and water. Cover and cook for 20 minutes. Remove garlic. Put mixture through a sieve or blend in blender. Add to stock and bring to boiling. Beat yolks with cream. Stir small amount hot soup into egg mixture; gradually return to hot soup, stirring as you add. Cook and stir 1 minute. Correct seasonings. Makes 6 servings.

CREAM OF AVOCADO

4 cups Cream of Chicken
    Stock (p. 13)
1 avocado, peeled and pitted

1 egg yolk, slightly beaten
¼ teaspoon salt
White pepper

Purée avocado by pressing through a sieve or food mill. Mix with egg yolk to thicken avocado. Heat Cream of Chicken Stock. Stir 1 cup hot stock into the avocado. Mix well. Gradually return to remaining stock, stirring as you add. Cook and stir 1 minute. Season with salt and white pepper. Makes 6 servings.

CREAM OF WATERCRESS

2 bunches watercress
3 tablespoons butter
4 cups Cream of Chicken
    Stock (p. 13)

Salt
White pepper
1 cup White Stock,
    Chicken (p. 12)

½ cup light cream

Trim and wash watercress. Reserve ¼ cup leaves. Simmer remainder in butter about 10 minutes. Add Cream of Chicken Stock and simmer 10 minutes longer. Put mixture through a sieve or blend in blender. Return to saucepan. Season with salt and white pepper. Add Chicken Stock and heat to boiling. Stir in cream and reserved watercress leaves. Reheat. Pour into tureen. Serve with croutons. Makes 6 servings.

CREAM OF MUSHROOM

1½ cups fresh mushrooms	2 egg yolks
2 tablespoons butter	2 tablespoons light cream
1 clove garlic, pressed	Salt
1 recipe Sauce Béchamel (p. 13)	White pepper
White Stock, Chicken (p. 12)	Chopped chives

Chop or grind mushrooms. Melt butter and add garlic. Add mushrooms and sauté 7 or 8 minutes. Make Sauce Béchamel and add mushroom mixture. Thin to desired thickness with stock. Just before serving, heat. Beat egg yolks with cream. Stir small amount hot soup into egg mixture; gradually return to hot soup, stirring as you add. Cook and stir 1 minute. Season with salt and white pepper. Garnish with chopped chives. Serve with Curry Rolls (p. 53). Makes 6 servings.

FRENCH CREAM OF POTATO AND ONION

3 large potatoes, pared and sliced	2 tablespoons flour
	1½ teaspoons salt
1 cup chopped leeks or green onions	¼ teaspoon pepper
	4 cups milk
2 tablespoons butter	Snipped parsley
Snipped chives	

Cook potatoes and leeks together in boiling salted water until tender. Drain, mash, and put through sieve or blend in blender. Melt butter in saucepan over low heat. Blend in flour, salt, and pepper. Cook over low heat, stirring until mixture is smooth and bubbly. Remove from heat. Gradually stir in milk. Heat to boiling, stirring constantly. Cook and stir 1 minute. Stir in potato mixture. Reheat. Correct seasonings. Garnish with parsley and chives. Makes 6 servings.

CREAM OF CAULIFLOWER

1 small head cauliflower	White Stock, Chicken (p. 12) or milk
1½ quarts Cream of Chicken Stock (p. 13)	2 tablespoons light cream
2 egg yolks	Chopped parsley or chives

Separate cauliflower into pieces and parboil for 8 minutes in salted water. Drain. Simmer cauliflower in Cream of Chicken Stock until fork-tender. Press cauliflower mixture through sieve or blend in blender. Return to saucepan. Thin with Chicken Stock or milk if too thick; heat. Beat egg yolks with cream. Stir small amount hot soup into egg mixture; gradually return to hot soup, stirring as you add. Cook and stir 1 minute. Correct seasonings. Garnish with parsley or chives. Makes 6 servings.

CREAM OF CELERY

1½ cups celery, sliced	2 egg yolks
1½ quarts Cream of	2 tablespoons light cream
Chicken Stock (p. 13)	Sliced radishes
Shredded lettuce	

Parboil celery in salted water. Drain. Add Cream of Chicken Stock and simmer until celery is tender. Press mixture through a sieve or blend in blender. Return soup to saucepan; heat. Beat egg yolks with cream. Stir small amount hot soup into egg mixture; gradually return to hot soup, stirring as you add. Cook and stir 1 minute. Correct seasonings. Garnish with sliced radishes and shredded lettuce. Makes 6 servings.

DINNER-IN-A-BOWL

FRENCH ONION SOUP

3 large onions, sliced	2 quarts Brown Stock (p. 11)
2 tablespoons butter	¼ cup dry sherry
2 teaspoons sugar	Day-old French bread, sliced
1 tablespoon flour	Grated Parmesan cheese

Sauté onions in butter 5 minutes. Sprinkle with sugar and sauté until onions are very brown and sugar is caramelized. Sprinkle with flour and continue to brown. Remove from heat. Gradually stir in stock. Heat to boiling, stirring constantly. Simmer 15 minutes. Correct seasonings. Just before serving, stir in sherry. Top each bowl of soup with a slice of day-old French bread and sprinkle with cheese. (If desired, the bowls may be put under the broiler to melt cheese. This is known as French Onion Soup Gratine.) Makes 8 servings.

It is said that Minestrone is not Minestrone until the spoon stands up straight in the soup.

MINESTRONE

2 onions, chopped	½ teaspoon basil
4 stalks celery, cut up	½ teaspoon oregano
3 zucchini, sliced	2 quarts Brown Stock (p. 11)
2 cloves garlic, pressed	3 (16 oz.) cans beans, (choose an
3 tablespoons olive oil	assortment: fava, kidney, Great
1 (6 oz.) can tomato paste	Northern, lima or pinto)
1 cup water	Sliced Pepperoni sausage,
Salt	if desired
¼ teaspoon crushed red	Cooked pasta (macaroni, shells,
pepper, if desired	or farfella), if desired

Parmesan cheese

Sauté onion, celery, zucchini and garlic in olive oil. Do not brown. Add tomato paste and water. Simmer 10 minutes. Add salt and crushed red pepper to taste. Add basil, oregano, stock, and beans. Cook about 15 minutes, stirring often. Add sliced Pepperoni, if desired. If soup is to be served as a main course, you may add cooked pasta. Garnish with Parmesan cheese and serve with bread sticks. (The long, thin bread sticks called grissinni are very good.) Makes 8 to 10 servings.

In making old-fashioned vegetable soup, vegetables were often put in with the meat and cooked a long time. This method destroys much of the flavor and most of the vitamins. The new way is much preferred.

NEW-FASHIONED NEW ENGLAND VEGETABLE SOUP

1½ cups White Stock, Chicken (p. 12)	3 turnips, cut julienne-style
½ cup uncooked rice	2 onions, minced
6 carrots, sliced	5 medium potatoes, cubed
	4 quarts strong Brown Stock (p. 11)

Cook rice in Chicken stock 15 minutes. Add rice mixture, carrots, turnips, onions, and potatoes to Brown stock. (Other vegetables may be added according to individual preference.) Simmer slowly about 30 to 40 minutes, until vegetables are cooked, but not too tender. Correct seasonings. Serve in large bowls with toasted crackers. Makes 8 servings.

LAMB AND VEGETABLE SOUP

1 small onion, chopped	½ soup can water
3 tablespoons salad oil	⅛ teaspoon rosemary
1 pound lamb, cubed	1 cup celery, sliced
1 (10½ oz.) can condensed beef consommé	2 potatoes, pared and cubed
	1 pound fresh green peas, cooked

Sauté onion in oil about 5 minutes. Add lamb and brown well. Add ½ can only of consommé, and the ½ soup can water. Cook until tender. Skim off fat, then add remaining consommé, rosemary, and celery. Cook about 10 minutes. Add potatoes and cook until tender. Add peas. Heat. Add more consommé if necessary. Makes 4 servings.

GUMBO FILÉ WITH SHRIMP

4 tablespoons oil

6 stalks celery, sliced

1 green pepper, cubed

1 onion, chopped

2 cloves garlic, pressed

6 parsley stems

2 quarts Ham Stock (p. 12)

4 fresh tomatoes, chopped

1 (6 oz.) can tomato paste

1 tablespoon sugar

1 tablespoon salt

¼ teaspoon pepper

1 tablespoon Creole seasoning
   (use amount to taste)

Fresh okra, sliced

2 pounds cooked shrimp
   or crab meat

1 tablespoon filé powder

3 cups hot cooked rice

Heat oil and sauté celery, pepper, onion, garlic, and parsley 3 minutes. Add ham stock, tomatoes, tomato paste, sugar, salt, pepper and seasoning. Simmer 20 minutes. Add okra; cook 10 minutes. Add cooked shrimp or crab; heat. Remove from heat. Add filé powder and stir gently. Place fluffy rice in large soup bowls and ladle gumbo over it. French bread, spread with garlic butter and toasted, is good to serve with this. Makes 6 servings.

BORSCHT

10 fresh beets, pared
   and chopped

2 cups Brown Stock (p. 11)

1 onion, sliced

1 bay leaf

4 parsley stems

¼ teaspoon thyme

¼ teaspoon marjoram

Salt

Pepper

1 or 2 tablespoons sugar

2 tablespoons vinegar

6 Polish sausages, sliced

Dairy sour cream

Chopped chives

Cook beets slowly in 1½ cups stock. Add onion, bay leaf, parsley, herbs, salt, and pepper. Continue cooking slowly for 30 minutes. Strain. Add sugar and vinegar and more salt if necessary. Adjust seasonings to taste. Cook sausage slices in ½ cup stock and add to soup. Pour hot soup into bowls and top each serving with a dollop of sour cream. Sprinkle with chopped chives. Serve with thinly sliced dark rye bread spread with chive butter and baked until crisp. Makes 6 servings.

FARMER'S SOUP

½ pound cabbage, shredded
½ pound kohlrabi, pared and
cut in strips
2 carrots, scraped and cut
in thick slices
½ pound green beans
1 cup fresh green peas

4 tablespoons butter
1 onion, minced
4 tablespoons flour
3 quarts White Stock, Chicken
(p. 12) and Vegetable Stock (p. 11)
½ teaspoon salt
¼ teaspoon pepper

Cook all vegetables separately in salted water. Drain, reserving the liquid. Combine vegetables and set aside. Melt butter and sauté onion until slightly brown. Stir in flour. Cook over low heat, stirring until mixture is bubbly. Remove from heat. Gradually stir in combined stocks. Heat to boiling, stirring constantly. Simmer 20 minutes. Add cooked vegetables and heat. Taste for seasoning. Serve with toasted rye bread. Makes 8 servings.

GOULASH SOUP

1 onion, diced
2 tablespoons oil
1 green pepper, diced
1 teaspoon paprika
1 pound beef, cubed
Salt
Pepper

2 tablespoons vinegar
½ (6 oz.) can tomato paste
1 tablespoon caraway seeds
½ teaspoon marjoram
1 clove garlic, pressed
2 quarts Brown Stock (p. 11)
3 potatoes, pared and diced

Sauté onion in oil until golden. Add green pepper and sauté 3 minutes. Sprinkle with paprika and sauté 1 minute. Add beef and stir well. Let meat brown slightly. Sprinkle with salt, pepper, and vinegar. Stir in the tomato paste. Simmer 4 minutes. Add seasonings and stock. Heat to boiling, then simmer 45 minutes or until meat is well done. Add potatoes and cook 10 to 15 minutes. This soup is delicious served with toasted light ryebread. Makes 6 servings.

OXTAIL SOUP

1 package oxtails	2 carrots, sliced
Salt	2 stalks celery, sliced
Pepper	4 parsley stems
Flour	1 bay leaf
2 tablespoons cooking oil	2 quarts Brown Stock (p. 11)
1 onion, diced	1 teaspoon lemon juice

1 teaspoon Worcestershire sauce

Wash oxtails and sponge dry. Season with salt and pepper. Roll in flour and sauté in oil. Transfer to soup pot. Add next 3 vegetables, parsley stems, and bay leaf. Add stock. Heat to boiling, cover, and simmer 2 to 3 hours or until meat is well-cooked. Lift out meat and strain broth. Remove all grease from broth by adding a tray of ice cubes and removing them immediately with a slotted spoon. If desired, more stock may be added. Then, while soup is being reheated, cook additional carrots and celery and add to soup. When soup is very hot and ready to serve, add lemon juice and Worcestershire sauce. This soup is good served with bread sticks. Makes 6 to 8 servings.

Pot-au-Feu is, as the French say, "a pot of fire which fills two plates." It is a popular dish in France and is served in many homes on Sunday. The bouillon is perhaps the richest and tastiest made.

POT-AU-FEU

4 pounds beef (brisket or chuck)	3 whole cloves
	2 leeks, sliced
1 chicken, if desired	1 onion, minced
3 quarts water or Brown Stock (p. 11)	5 stalks celery, sliced
	6 carrots, cubed
1 teaspoon salt	1 medium rutabaga, pared and cubed
¼ teaspoon pepper	
½ teaspoon thyme	1 medium cabbage, cubed
1 bay leaf	2 parsnips, pared and cubed

Cover the meat with water, bring to a boil, and cook 5 minutes. Remove meat and discard water. Rinse the pot. Return meat to pot and add salt. Add water or stock. Add seasonings. Heat to boiling, skimming off fat if necessary. Cover and simmer 1½ hours. Add vegetables and cook about 45 minutes or until vegetables are fork-tender. Remove meat and vegetables and keep warm. Strain broth through a cheesecloth and serve broth as a first course. Slice meat and arrange with the vegetables on a platter; serve as the main course. (Small boiled potatoes are often added to the platter.) Makes 8 servings.

CHICKEN NOODLE SOUP

4 to 5-pound stewing chicken, cut up
1 onion, chopped
3 stalks celery, cut up
2 carrots, cut up
4 parsley stems
2 teaspoons salt
6 whole peppercorns
1 (8 oz.) package medium noodles, or Homemade Noodles (p. 52)
Cooked carrots, celery, and peas, if desired
Snipped parsley

Wash chicken; remove any excess pieces of fat. Place in kettle with giblets and neck. Add enough water to cover. Add vegetables, parsley, salt, and peppercorns. Heat to boiling. Reduce heat; cover and simmer 2½ to 3½ hours, or until thickest pieces are fork-tender. Remove chicken and strain the broth. Cool broth; skim off fat. Remove meat from bones and skin; slice. Cook noodles in boiling salted water; drain. When ready to serve, add noodles and sliced meat to soup; heat. If desired, cooked carrots, celery, and peas may be added to make a heartier soup. Pour into tureen and garnish with snipped parsley. Makes 8 to 10 servings.

HOT AND HEARTY FAVORITES

NAVY BEAN SOUP

1 pound dried navy beans	1 teaspoon butter
2 quarts water	½ teaspoon savory
2 teaspoons salt	Freshly ground pepper to taste
1 carrot, cut up	1 meaty ham bone or ham hock
1 onion, cut up	1 cup potatoes, diced
Chopped parsley	

Rinse and sort beans. Soak overnight in water to cover and drain. (Or simmer 2 minutes and soak covered 1 hour; drain.) Put beans in soup pot and add water and salt; heat to boiling. Sauté carrot and onion in butter and add to beans. Add the savory, pepper, and meat. Cover and cook slowly about 2 to 3 hours, adding potatoes the last hour. Remove meat. Remove about 1 cup beans and put through sieve or blend in blender. Return to pot. Cut meat in pieces, remove fat, and return meat to soup. Correct seasonings. Heat well and sprinkle with chopped parsley. Serve with toasted Corn Bread (p. 53). Makes 6 servings.

"Groene Erwtensoep," or Dutch Pea Soup, is perhaps the most famous of all Dutch dishes.

DUTCH PEA SOUP

2 cups dried green peas	3 quarts water
3 onions, sliced	3 potatoes, pared and diced
Salt	3 ham sausages
1 pound ham hock or ham bone	1 cup fresh peas, cooked

Soak dried peas overnight in water. Drain and rinse. Place dried peas, onions, salt, and meat in soup pot with 3 quarts water. Cover and cook slowly about 3 hours. Fifteen minutes before peas are done, add diced potatoes. Cook the sausages and slice. Just before serving, add green peas and sausage slices. Heat. Makes 8 servings.

TURNIP AND POTATO SOUP

3 turnips, pared and minced	5 cups water
3 potatoes, pared and minced	2 tablespoons butter
1 teaspoon salt	1½ cups milk
Snipped parsley	

Place turnips, potatoes, salt, water, and 1 tablespoon butter in saucepan. Heat to boiling; cook 2 hours or until potatoes are tender. Remove from heat and mash or blend. Add milk. Heat to boiling. Correct seasonings. Add remaining butter. Sprinkle with snipped parsley. Makes 4 or 5 servings.

LENTIL SOUP

2 cups dried lentils	Snipped parsley
1 onion, chopped	Chopped mint leaves
1 tablespoon ham drippings	Cooked frankfurters, sliced,
1 bay leaf	if desired
¼ teaspoon thyme	1 fresh tomato, chopped, if desired
5 parsley stems	

Sort and rinse lentils. Soak overnight in water to cover. Drain and rinse. Sauté the onion in the ham drippings. Put lentils in soup pot and add onion, bay leaf, thyme, and parsley stems. Add water to cover. Heat to boiling; cover and simmer about 1½ hours. Correct seasonings. Discard bay leaf and parsley stems. Just before serving, add freshly chopped parsley and mint leaves. If desired, garnish each bowl with slices of frankfurters and chopped tomato. Serve with sesame crackers. Makes 8 servings.

MULLIGATAWNY

3-pound chicken, cut up	2 teaspoons curry powder
Butter	4 quarts White Stock, Chicken (p. 12)
2 carrots, cut up	1 tablespoon sugar
½ green pepper, cut up	Salt and pepper
2 tart apples, cut up	3 medium fresh tomatoes
1 tablespoon flour	3 cups hot cooked rice

In soup pot, brown the chicken pieces in butter. Remove chicken and add carrot, green pepper and apple. Cook 5 minutes. Mix flour and curry and sprinkle over mixture. Stir well. Gradually stir in stock. Heat to boiling, stirring constantly. Season with sugar, salt, and pepper. Add chicken and cook until done. Add tomato. Cook 15 minutes. Remove chicken and cut off meat. Strain soup, pressing vegetables and apples through sieve. Add chicken meat. Heat well. Serve in bowls over fluffy rice. Makes 6 servings.

MEXICAN BEAN SOUP

1 pound pinto beans

1 onion

2 tablespoons cooking oil

2 quarts Brown Stock (p. 11)

2 cloves garlic on wooden picks

1 green pepper, finely chopped

1 sweet red pepper, finely chopped

2 dried hot peppers

Salt to taste

¼ teaspoon oregano

Hard-cooked egg, sliced

Lime slices

Sort and rinse beans. Soak overnight in cold water. Drain and rinse. Place in soup pot; cover with water. Cover and simmer about 2 hours. Drain, reserving 2 cups bean liquid. In soup pot, sauté the onion in oil. Add beans, bean liquid, stock, garlic, and peppers. Heat to boiling. Add salt and oregano. Simmer about 1 hour. Remove garlic and dried red peppers. Often the soup is strained and the beans puréed and simmered an additional 15 minutes. When serving, garnish each bowl with a slice of hard-cooked egg and a slice of lime. Serve with corn chips. Makes 6 servings.

HAM AND CELERY CABBAGE SOUP

½ cup onion, chopped

½ cup celery, chopped

½ cup green pepper, chopped

2 tablespoons butter

6 cups White Stock, Chicken (p. 12)

1 celery cabbage, shredded

3 cups cooked ham, cubed

1 bay leaf

½ teaspoon salt

⅛ teaspoon pepper

¾ cup dairy sour cream

¼ cup dry sherry, if desired

2 tablespoons parsley, chopped

Sauté onion, celery, and green pepper in butter until clear. Set aside. Heat stock. Add cabbage, ham, bay leaf, salt, pepper, and sautéed vegetable mixture. Cook 10 minutes or until cabbage is tender. Remove bay leaf. Just before serving, add sour cream, mixing well. Heat slightly. Add dry sherry, if desired, and sprinkle with parsley. Makes 8 servings.

GARBANZO (CHICK–PEA) SOUP

2 quarts strong White Stock, Chicken (p. 12)

½ teaspoon saffron

2 potatoes, pared and cubed

2 (16 oz.) cans garbanzo beans

½ green pepper, cut in squares

2 fresh tomatoes, cut up

Heat stock to boiling and add saffron, potatoes, and garbanzos. Cook until potatoes are tender. Just before serving, add green pepper and tomatoes. Reheat. Serve with corn sticks or crusty French rolls. Makes 6 to 8 servings.

GAME SOUP

1 pheasant, partridge, or duck

2 tablespoons salad oil

2 quarts White Stock, Chicken (p.12)

3 carrots, scraped

1 onion, chopped

3 stalks celery

Salt

Pepper

Juniper berries

Sage or marjoram

Remove breast of bird; set aside. Place oil in soup kettle and brown remainder of bird well. Add stock, carrots, onion, and celery. Add salt, pepper, juniper berries, and bay leaf. Heat to boiling and simmer until broth is flavored. Skim as necessary. Meanwhile, sauté breasts in butter and cook slowly until tender. Cut cooked breast meat in cubes or julienne strips. Strain broth through a cheesecloth and correct seasonings. Discard vegetables and bones. Add breast to broth; heat. Makes 8 servings.

This delicious soup is served daily in the United States Senate dining room.

UNITED STATES SENATE BEAN SOUP

1 pound dried Great Northern beans

3 quarts water

1 or 2 ham hocks

1 onion studded with 5 cloves

3 stalks celery

2 cloves garlic on wooden picks

Salt

Pepper

1 cup mashed potatoes

2 tablespoons snipped parsley

Soak beans overnight in cold water. Drain and rinse. Place in kettle with water and ham hocks. Heat to boiling; cover and simmer 2 hours. Add onion, celery, garlic, salt, and pepper. Simmer 1 hour longer. Remove garlic. Remove ham hocks and cut off meat. Add potatoes and meat; heat well. Correct seasonings. Pour into soup tureen and sprinkle with parsley. Serve with oven-toasted whole wheat bread. Makes 6 to 8 servings.

POTAGES

A potage is a thick, hearty soup made from simple ingredients. Any potage will serve as a filling, nutritious main course for a meal.

CORN CHOWDER

2 slices salt pork, or
   2 tablespoons butter
1 tablespoon onion, chopped
1 cup diced potatoes, cooked
     Parsley, chopped

2 cups fresh corn, cut off the cob
2 cups milk
Salt
Pepper

If salt pork is used, cut in cubes; sauté until crisp. Remove salt pork and reserve. Add onion to pork fat or butter in skillet and sauté. Add cooked potatoes, corn, milk, and seasonings. Heat well. Just before serving, add the reserved pork bits. (A can of crab meat may be added to make a most elegant luncheon soup.) Garnish with chopped parsley. Serve with cheese-flavored popcorn. Makes 4 servings.

POTAGE ST. GERMAIN

2 tablespoons onion, chopped
2 tablespoons butter
2½ cups fresh green peas
1 carrot, sliced
1 tablespoon snipped parsley
3 lettuce leaves
     Croutons

1 teaspoon sugar
Salt
White pepper
2½ cups White Stock, Chicken (p. 12)
1 cup heavy cream
Snipped parsley

Sauté onion in butter. Add peas, carrot, 1 tablespoon parsley, lettuce, sugar, salt, pepper, and stock. Cook until vegetables are very soft. Put through sieve or blend in blender. Stir in cream and heat slowly. Sprinkle with parsley. Pass croutons. Serve with toasted, buttered English muffins. Makes 4 servings.

POTAGE MONDAY

3 carrots	1 tablespoon butter
3 stalks celery	½ cup White Stock, Chicken (p. 12)
2 turnips, pared	1½ quarts Potage St. Germain (p. 31)

Cut carrots, celery, and turnips into matchsticks 1 inch long. Sauté in butter. Add stock and cook until tender. Add Potage St. Germain. Heat well. Serve with bread crusts. Makes 6 servings.

CREAM OF TOMATO SOUP

1 onion, chopped	2 cups fresh tomatoes, chopped,
1 carrot, chopped	peeled
2 tablespoons butter	Salt to taste
3 tablespoons flour	White pepper to taste
1 quart White Stock, Chicken (p. 12)	1 tablespoon sugar
1 cup evaporated milk	

Sauté onion and carrot in butter. Add flour and mix well. Cook and stir over low heat. Remove from heat. Gradually stir in stock. Heat to boiling, stirring constantly. Cook and stir 1 minute. Add tomatoes, salt, white pepper, and sugar. Cover and simmer about 1 hour. Put mixture through sieve or blend in blender. Stir in evaporated milk. Heat but do not boil. If soup is too thick, add a little more stock. Makes 4 or 5 servings.

POTAGE AURORE

3 carrots	2 tablespoons butter
3 stalks celery	½ cup White Stock, Chicken (p. 12)
2 turnips, pared	1 quart Potage St. Germain (p. 31)
1 quart Cream of Tomato Soup (p. 32)	

Cut carrots, celery, and turnips into cubes. Sauté in butter. Add stock and cook until tender. Add Potage St. Germain and Cream of Tomato Soup. Heat and serve. Makes 6 to 8 servings.

ESSENCE OF MUSHROOM SOUP

½ pound fresh mushrooms, sliced	4 cups White Stock, Chicken (p. 12)
1 small onion, chopped	½ teaspoon salt
3 tablespoons butter	2 tablespoons dry sherry
Mimosa Garnish (p. 33)	

Sauté sliced mushrooms and onion in butter 4 minutes. Place in blender with 1 cup stock. Blend 7 seconds. Pour into saucepan and add remaining stock and salt. Simmer 10 minutes. Add sherry and serve very hot with Mimosa Garnish (p. 33). Makes 4 servings.

For an interesting way to serve a familiar vegetable, try Cream of Broccoli Soup, page 17. It's a nutritious cold weather appetite-teaser.

Asparagus is a versatile vegetable when served alone or in a soup. As a delightful first course to a sit-down dinner try Asparagus Vinaigrette, page 72.

...ess up an old favorite, Cream of Celery Soup, page 20, with any ...ndwich for a hot and hearty lunch.

Either fresh, frozen or canned vegetables in a hearty meat stock make a delicious vegetable soup. Be sure to try several recipes from the Dinner-In-A-Bowl section like a good tasty Minestrone, page 21.

MIMOSA GARNISH

2 hard-cooked eggs   **¼ cup snipped parsley**

Chop the egg whites and put yolks through a sieve. Combine with parsley.

POTAGE FLORENTINE

3 cups fresh peas	3 cups White Stock, Chicken (p. 12)
2 cups carrots, sliced	Salt
½ pound fresh spinach	Pepper
¼ cup butter	1 cup evaporated milk
¼ cup flour	Chives, chopped
	Parsley, chopped

Cook peas uncovered in small amount of boiling salted water for 5 minutes; cook covered 3 to 7 minutes. Drain peas, reserving ½ cup liquid. Cook carrots covered in boiling salted water 12 to 15 minutes. Drain, reserving ¼ cup liquid. Cook spinach covered 3 minutes, using only the water clinging to leaves. Place reserved cooking liquids, peas, carrots, and spinach in a blender and blend. Melt butter in saucepan; blend in flour. Cook over low heat until mixture is smooth and bubbly. Remove from heat. Gradually stir in stock. Heat to boiling, stirring constantly. Cook and stir 1 minute. Add salt and pepper to taste. Remove from heat; add evaporated milk. Heat. Garnish with chopped chives and parsley. Serve with toasted English muffins. Makes 4 servings.

POTAGE OF PUMPKIN

3 pounds pumpkin	½ teaspoon ginger
½ small onion, chopped	¼ teaspoon nutmeg
3 tablespoons butter	White pepper
3 tablespoons flour	2 egg yolks
4½ cups White Stock, Chicken (p. 12)	2 tablespoons light cream
	Snipped parsley
1 teaspoon salt	

Halve pumpkin; remove seeds and stringy portion. Cut pumpkin into small pieces and pare. Cook covered in 1 inch bowling salted water 25 to 30 minutes or until tender. Sauté chopped onion in butter; blend in flour. Cook over low heat, stirring until mixture is bubbly. Remove from heat. Stir in pumpkin purée, stock, salt, ginger, nutmeg, and white pepper. Heat to boiling, stirring constantly. Cook and stir 1 minute. Mix egg yolks and cream. Stir small amount hot soup into egg mixture; gradually return to soup, stirring as you add. Garnish with parsley. Serve with Pulled Bread (p. 54). Makes 4 servings.

POTAGE RED MOUNTAIN

3 carrots, coarsely chopped	½ teaspoon basil
3 potatoes, coarsely chopped	Dash sugar
3 fresh tomatoes, peeled	Salt
and quartered	Pepper
2 tablespoons butter	Chopped chives
8 cups boiling water	Dairy sour cream

Sauté carrots, potatoes, and tomatoes 3 minutes in butter. Add boiling water, basil, and sugar. Add salt and pepper to taste. Simmer about 1 hour or until vegetables are tender. Put mixture through a sieve or blend in blender. Return to saucepan; heat. Top with chopped chives and a dollop of sour cream. Makes 6 servings.

LIMA BEAN AND MUSHROOM CHOWDER

¼ cup chopped salt pork	1 package frozen lima beans
1 onion, chopped	Salt
1 quart White Stock, Chicken (p. 12)	Pepper
2 cups carrots, cubed	Nutmeg
2 cups potatoes, pared, cubed	2 cups light cream
1 cup fresh mushrooms, sliced	2 tablespoons butter
Shredded lettuce, if desired	

Sauté salt pork 3 to 4 minutes. Add chopped onion and sauté until onion is tender. Add stock, carrots, potatoes, mushrooms, and lima beans. Add salt, pepper, and nutmeg to taste. Cover and simmer about 20 minutes. Add cream and cook for 5 minutes longer. Just before serving, heat soup and add butter. (The butter gives the soup a shine.) A little shredded lettuce may be added as a garnish just before serving. Makes 4 servings.

POTAGE OF CARROT

4 carrots, minced

1 onion, chopped

3 tablespoons butter

1 quart plus 2 cups White
    Stock, Chicken (p. 12)

½ cup uncooked regular rice

1 tablespoon sugar

1 teaspoon salt

1 cup evaporated milk

Crusts of French bread

Snipped parsley

Sauté carrots and onion in 2 tablespoons of butter. Cover and cook slowly 5 minutes. Add 1 quart stock, rice, sugar, and salt. Simmer 15 minutes. Put mixture tthrough a sieve or blend in blender; return to pan. Add the 2 cups stock and bring to boiling. Remove from heat. Stir in evaporated milk and the remaining tablespoon butter. Heat. Serve from tureen with crusts of French bread and a sprinkle of parsley floating on top. Makes 4 servings.

POTAGE TOMATO

2 carrots, chopped

2 onions, chopped

¼ cup butter

¾ cup flour

2 cups White Stock, Chicken (p. 12)

2 (16 oz.) cans Italian tomatoes,
    puréed

4 fresh tomatoes, peeled
    and chopped

2 stalks celery, cut up

1 tablespoon sugar

White pepper

1 teaspoon basil

1 cup evaporated milk or more,
    if desired

Salt

Sauté carrots and onions in butter about 5 minutes. Stir in flour. Cook and stir over low heat 2 minutes. Remove from heat. Gradually stir in stock. Heat to boiling, stirring constantly. Cook and stir 1 minute. Add puréed Italian tomatoes, fresh tomatoes, celery, sugar, white pepper, and basil. Cover and simmer 2 hours. Put mixture through sieve or blend in blender. Return to pan. Just before serving, heat slowly and add evaporated milk. Add salt to taste. If soup is too thick, add more milk. Makes 4 servings.

CREAM OF TOMATO NEOPOLITAN

1½ quarts of Potage Tomato (p. 35) ½ (8 oz.) box fine spaghetti

Cook spaghetti in boiling salted water until fork-tender. Drain. Cut in 1 inch lengths and add to Potage Tomato. Makes 6 servings.

CREAM OF TOMATO PORTUGUESE

¾ cup hot cooked rice   1½ quarts Potage Tomato (p. 35)
Chopped basil

Add cooked rice to Potage Tomato and sprinkle with chopped basil. Makes 6 servings.

OYSTER STEW

1½ quarts milk   ¼ teaspoon paprika
1 pint fresh oysters   ⅛ teaspoon pepper
3 tablespoons butter   ½ teaspoon salt
1 teaspoon Worcestershire   2 tablespoons butter
  sauce, if desired

Scald milk. Drain oysters, reserving liquid. Cook oysters in 3 tablespoons butter over low heat just until edges curl. Add reserved liquid to milk. Add oysters, Worcestershire sauce, if desired, paprika, and pepper. Heat slowly but do not boil. Add salt. Put a little butter in each soup plate before ladling in soup. Serve with oyster crackers. Makes 6 servings.

NEW ENGLAND CLAM CHOWDER

2 (7-8 oz.) cans clams,   2 large potatoes, pared and diced
  minced (to use fresh clams,   2 onions, minced
  see instructions (p. 37)   2 cups milk
¼ pound salt pork, diced   1 tablespoon butter
1 quart water   Salt and pepper to taste

Drain clams, reserving liquid. In large saucepan, fry salt pork until crisp. Remove pork and reserve. Add water, reserved clam liquid, potatoes, and onions to fat in saucepan. Cook covered until potatoes are tender, about 15 to 20 minutes. Add clams, milk, 1 tablespoon butter, and seasonings to taste. Reheat to serving temperature. Top each serving with pork pieces and pat of butter. Serve with pilot crackers. Makes 6 servings.

MANHATTAN-STYLE CLAM CHOWDER

2 (7-8 oz.) cans clams, minced
  (to substitute fresh clams, see
  instructions below)

¼ pound salt pork, diced

1 onion, minced

2 potatoes, pared and cubed

4 fresh tomatoes, peeled
  and chopped

1 stalk celery, diced

5 cups water

1 bay leaf

Pinch thyme

Salt and pepper to taste

Drain clams, reserving liquid. In large saucepan, fry salt pork until crisp. Add onion and cook until transparent. Add potatoes, tomatoes, celery, water, bay leaf, thyme, and reserved clam liquid. Cover; simmer 30 minutes. Add salt, pepper, and clams. Reheat to serving temperature. Serve with pilot crackers. Makes 8 servings.

To use fresh clams steamed in the shell: Wash 2 to 3 dozen clams. Cover with salt water (⅓ cup salt to 1 gallon cold water); let stand 15 minutes. Rinse. Repeat twice. Place rinsed clams in large kettle. Add 1 cup water; cover and steam just until shells open, 5 to 10 minutes. Remove clams, reserving liquid. Remove shells; dice clams. Strain liquid. Use clams and liquid as directed above.

CREAM OF SHRIMP SOUP

1 pound shrimp, cooked

3 cups milk

1 cup light cream

2 tablespoons flour

4 tablespoons butter

½ teaspoon salt

⅛ teaspoon pepper

1 cup fresh green peas, cooked

2 tablespoons dry sherry, if desired

Chop shrimp and add to milk in top of double boiler. Cook 30 minutes. Remove from heat. Put ½ cup cream and the flour in a shaker; shake until smooth. Gradually add flour mixture to milk. Heat until thickened, stirring constantly. Stir in remaining cream, butter, salt, pepper, and peas. Just before serving, add sherry. Makes 4 servings.

CIOPPINO

1 large striped bass
1 (2 lb.) live lobster, or 2
    frozen rock-lobster tails
    or 1 crab
1 pint clams, in the shell
½ cup olive oil
1 onion, minced
2 cloves garlic, pressed
3 tablespoons parsley, snipped
1 green pepper, chopped

½ pint fresh mushrooms
2 medium fresh tomatoes, peeled
    and cooked
1 bay leaf
2 whole cloves
1 cup red wine
Salt
Cayenne pepper
1 cup raw shrimp, shelled and
    deveined

Wash bass and cut into slices. Cut lobster or crab into pieces. Steam clams and reserve liquid. Heat oil in soup pot; add onion, garlic, parsley, green pepper, and mushrooms. Cook slowly 5 minutes. Add tomatoes, bay leaf, cloves, wine, and reserved clam liquid. Cover and simmer 1 hour. Season with salt and cayenne pepper to taste. Add fish, lobster or crab, and shrimp. Cook 15 minutes. Add clams and heat. Serve in heated bowls with Italian bread sticks. Makes 4 servings.

It is impossible in this country to make Bouillabaisse as it is made in France. The best we can do is make a good soup with the fish available. Like many dishes in France, this dish is two-in-one. In other words, the liquid, or bouillon, is drained off and served in a bowl, while the fish and seafood are served as a separate course. French bread is always sliced and placed in the bottom of the soup bowl with the soup ladled over it.

BOUILLABAISSE, AMERICAN-STYLE

1 pound raw fish, sliced
1 teaspoon curry powder
1 teaspoon lemon peel, grated
1 teaspoon Tabasco sauce
1 tablespoon snipped parsley
2 teaspoons salt
¼ teaspoon pepper
2 tablespoons butter
2 tablespoons flour

1 quart water or Fish Stock (p. 11)
1 onion, chopped
1 carrot, sliced
2 green peppers, sliced
1 fresh tomato, peeled and sliced
½ cup vinegar or wine
3 cloves garlic on wooden picks
1 bay leaf
French bread, sliced and toasted

Use at least two kinds of fish, but more if possible. (Halibut, bass, sea trout, cod, bluefish, and red snapper are possibilities.) Mix next 6 seasonings and rub into slices of fish. Melt butter; blend in flour. Cook over low heat, stirring until smooth and bubbly. Remove from heat. Gradually stir in water. Heat to boiling, stirring constantly. Cook and stir 1 minute. Add vegetables, vinegar or wine, garlic, and bay leaf. Bring to a boil and add fish. Cook slowly 20 to 30 minutes. Remove garlic. Place toast in tureen and pour hot broth over it. Serve fish as a separate course. (Both broth and fish may be ladled over the toast if desired, but separating them is much more authentic.) Makes 4 servings.

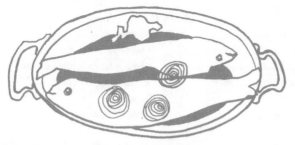

BOURRIDE

2 pounds fish (bass, haddock, or flounder)

1 onion, minced

Bouquet of herbs (cheesecloth bag of thyme, crumbled bay leaf, fennel, peel of ½ an orange, salt, and pepper)

Boiling water or Fish Stock (p. 11)

12 slices bread

Garlic

2 cups Aioli Sauce (p. 40)

Cut fish in serving pieces and place in soup pot. Cover with onion and herbs. Add boiling water or stock to just cover and simmer 10 minutes. While fish is cooking, toast the bread and rub well with garlic. Place in large tureen or platter. Prepare Aioli Sauce. When fish is cooked, remove and keep warm. Strain the broth and combine 3 cups of it, little by little, with 1 cup Aioli Sauce. Mix well but carefully. Put in saucepan over low heat or in double boiler and stir with wooden spoon until it coats the spoon. (It must not boil.) Pour this over the toast and serve the fish separately. Pass the remaining cup of Aioli Sauce. This soup is for the hardy ones, but it is truly an experience to serve and eat. Makes 6 servings.

AIOLI SAUCE

5 cloves garlic
1 egg yolk

2 tablespoons olive oil
1 cup mayonnaise

Press garlic in blender and add egg yolk. Blend. Add olive oil and blend. Add mayonnaise and blend 2 seconds to mix. This sauce is for the hardy ones, but the more you eat the more you like it. It may also be used as a dip for raw vegetables.

CRAB BISQUE

1 (8 oz.) package sole
1 recipe Court Bouillon (below)
White Stock, Chicken (p. 12)
1 (7½ oz.) can crab meat
Salt
Cayenne pepper

Nutmeg
2 teaspoons dry sherry
2 egg yolks, slightly beaten
½ cup whipped cream
Parsley
Lemon slices

Paprika

Poach sole in Court Bouillon, reserving bouillon. Measure bouillon; add stock to make 5 cups. Reserve a few pieces of crab meat and place the remainder in blender with 2 tablespoons stock. Blend. Remove and do the same with sole. Place both in saucepan with the bouillon. Heat to boiling. Add seasonings to taste. Stir sherry into egg yolks. Stir small amount hot bouillon into egg mixture; gradually return to bouillon, stirring as you add. Cook and stir 1 minute. To each serving, add reserved pieces of crab and top with slightly salted whipped cream. Garnish with parsley and lemon slices. Dust with paprika. Makes 4 to 6 servings.

COURT BOUILLON

1 cup white wine
1 carrot, cut up
3 sprigs parsley
½ teaspoon thyme
1 bay leaf

½ small onion, studded with
2 cloves
½ teaspoon salt
⅛ teaspoon pepper
1 cup boiling water

Place wine, carrot, parsley, thyme, bay leaf, onion, salt and pepper in saucepan. Add boiling water and boil mixture about 20 minutes. Strain before using.

SUMMER SOUPS

BEET SOUP

½ cup dried navy beans	2 tablespoons butter
6 medium fresh beets with tops	1 tart apple, chopped
1 small head cabbage, quartered	2 quarts Brown Stock (p. 11)
4 fresh tomatoes, peeled	½ teaspoon salt
and cut up	⅛ teaspoon pepper

6 tablespoons dairy sour cream

Rinse and sort beans. Soak overnight in water to cover, and drain. (Or simmer 2 minutes and soak covered 1 hour; drain.) Cover with water and cook until tender. Cook beets (see instructions below). Pour 3 quarts scalding hot water on cabbage. Sauté tomatoes in butter and put through a sieve. Add all vegetables and chopped apple to the stock and cook for 30 minutes. Season with salt and pepper. Pour the soup into hot soup plates and stir 1 tablespoon sour cream into each serving. Makes 6 servings.

How to cook beets: Cut off all but 2 inches of beet tops. Wash beets and leave whole with root ends attached. Combine 6 cups water, 1 tablespoon vinegar (to preserve color), and 1 teaspoon salt; heat to boiling. Add beets. Cover and cook 35 to 45 minutes or until tender. Drain. Run cold water over beets; slip off skins and remove root ends. Slice beets.

CREAM OF CUCUMBER SOUP

3 cucumbers	Dash cayenne pepper
8 medium green onions, sliced	3 tablespoons flour
3 cups cold water	1 tablespoon mint leaves, chopped
¼ teaspoon salt	½ cup light cream

Pare 2 cucumbers, leaving one unpared. Slice all three crosswise. Place in pan with green onions and 1 cup of water. Add salt and pepper.

Cook until vegetables are soft. Put ½ cup cold water and flour in shaker; shake until smooth. Gradually stir flour mixture into soup. Add remaining water. Heat to boiling, stirring constantly. Cook 10 minutes. Strain; stir in mint and cool. Stir in cream. Cover and chill well. Makes 4 servings.

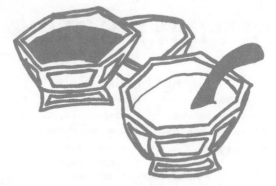

Vichyssoise is an American soup, not French, as many believe. A French chef in America made his famous "Soup Bon Femme," a potato and leek soup, and put the leftover soup in the refrigerator. The next day he added a little more cream, topped it with chives, and served it on a compote of chopped ice. He named the new soup, now one of our most popular summer favorites, for Vichy, his hometown in France.

VICHYSSOISE

2 potatoes, sliced

6 leeks or 12 medium green onions, sliced

1 stalk celery, sliced

1 onion, minced

2 tablespoons butter

2 cups White Stock, Chicken (p. 12)

3 sprigs parsley

½ teaspoon salt

Freshly ground pepper

Dash nutmeg

¼ teaspoon Worcestershire sauce

1 cup heavy cream

Snipped chives

Cook potatoes, leeks, celery, and onion in butter 10 minutes. Add stock and parsley; cover and simmer 30 minutes. Put mixture through a sieve or blend in blender. Pour into bowl or refrigerator container. Add salt, pepper, nutmeg, Worcestershire sauce, and cream. Stir to mix. Cover and chill well. Garnish with chives. Makes 4 servings.

Gazpacho is not really a soup or a salad. It is too thick to be a soup and too thin to be a salad, so just call it Gazpacho and serve it often.

GAZPACHO

4 fresh tomatoes, peeled and finely chopped

1 green pepper, finely chopped

2 cucumbers, chopped

1 onion, finely chopped

¼ cup olive oil

1 (46 oz.) can tomato juice

3 tablespoons wine vinegar

1 clove garlic, pressed

Snipped parsley

½ teaspoon basil

½ teaspoon salt

¼ teaspoon sugar

¼ teaspoon pepper

Fresh basil leaves, if desired

Combine chopped vegetables. (Do not use a blender to chop vegetables; they must have texture.) Add olive oil, tomato juice, vinegar, and next 6 seasonings. Cover and chill well. Correct seasonings. Place an ice cube in each chilled glass bowl and a leaf of basil, if desired. Ladle in the Gazpacho. Serve with crisp croutons. Makes 4 servings.

JELLIED MADRILENE

2 cups tomato purée

1 quart hot Chicken or Beef Consommé (p. 12)

Parsley

1 envelope unflavored gelatin

¼ cup cold beet juice

Lemon wedges

Boil the purée, reducing it to one-half its original volume. Add to consommé. Sprinkle gelatin on beet juice to soften. Dissolve in hot consommé. Chill. Beat with a fork and serve in chilled bouillon cups. Garnish with lemon wedges and parsley. Serve with freshly-made Melba toast. Makes 4 servings.

COLD SENEGALESE

3 cups White Stock, Chicken (p. 12)

1 cup chicken meat, finely chopped

½ teaspoon curry powder

4 egg yolks

2 cups evaporated milk

Avocado slices, not too ripe

Unpared apple, sliced

Heat stock to boiling and add chicken meat. Add curry powder. Beat egg yolks. Stir a small amount hot stock into eggs; blend with milk.

Add egg mixture to stock, stirring as you add. Cook and stir over low heat. Taste and correct seasonings. Cover and chill well. Garnish with slices of apple and avocado. Makes 4 servings.

FRUIT SOUP

2 pounds ripe Bing cherries, pitted
6 to 8 cherry pits, crushed
7 cups water
½ cup sugar
1 stick cinnamon
3 tablespoons lemon juice
4 tablespoons white wine
2 tablespoons cornstarch
½ cup white wine
Whipped cream, sweetened

Pit cherries over a bowl to save juice. Reserve 1 cup juice. Tie cherry pits in a cheesecloth and crush with a hammer. Cook cherries and bundle of crushed pits in water until cherries are soft. Remove pits and blend cherries in blender or put through a sieve. Combine cherries and juice; return to soup. Add sugar, cinnamon, and lemon juice. Correct seasonings. Blend cornstarch with 4 tablespoons white wine and add to soup. Cook, stirring constantly, until mixture thickens and boils. Cook and stir 1 minute. Remove cinnamon stick. Add remaining ½ cup wine. Check seasoning again. If soup is to be served warm, it is ready; otherwise chill at least 2 hours. Garnish with chopped fresh cherries and top with slightly sweetened whipped cream. Serve with toast. Makes 6 servings.

COLD CANTALOUPE SOUP

1 cantaloupe
⅓ cup butter
1 tablespoon sugar
⅛ teaspoon salt
1 lemon peel
3 cups milk

Remove meat of melon, dice 1 cup and save. Chop remaining melon. Melt butter and add chopped melon, sugar, salt, and lemon peel. Simmer 3 minutes. Add milk and bring to a boil. Simmer 10 minutes. Remove lemon peel. Put through a sieve or blend in blender. Chill. Garnish with diced melon. Serve with thin slices of buttered rye bread. Makes 4 servings.

BLENDER AVOCADO SOUP

1 ripe avocado, peeled
   and pitted
1½ cups White Stock,
   Chicken (p. 12)
1 tablespoon lemon juice

Salt
Pepper
Cayenne pepper
1 cup light cream
Lemon slices

Blend avocado, stock, and lemon juice until smooth. Add salt, pepper, and cayenne pepper to taste. Add cream. Cover and chill well. Stir well and garnish with lemon slices. Makes 4 servings.

COMBINATION SOUPS

CREAM CLARMART

1 (11 oz.) can condensed Green
    Pea Soup
1 (10½ oz.) can condensed Cream
    of Chicken Soup

2 (13 oz.) cans evaporated milk
1 cup fresh green peas, cooked
¼ head lettuce, shredded

Place soups and milk in blender, a little of each at a time, and blend. Pour into saucepan. Add peas. Heat slowly. Just before serving, add the lettuce. Serve with parsley-buttered toasted crackers. Makes 4 servings.

BOMBAY SOUP

2 whole carrots
1 stalk celery
1 small onion, cut up
2 cups White Stock, Chicken (p. 12)
2 (10½ oz.) cans condensed
    Cream of Chicken Soup

1 cup fresh green peas, cooked
½ cup evaporated milk
2 teaspoons curry powder
2 tablespoons dry sherry,
    if desired
Whipped cream, if desired

Cook carrots, celery, and onion in stock until carrots are tender. Remove vegetables; discard celery and onion. Dice the carrots. Mix the stock with chicken soup; blend in blender until smooth. Return to saucepan. Add diced carrots and the peas. Gradually stir milk into curry powder; stir into soup. Add sherry. Heat. Top with whipped cream. Makes 4 servings.

EASY BOUILLABAISSE

1 (11 oz.) can condensed Green
  Pea Soup
1 (10½ oz.) can condensed
  Tomato Soup
1 cup light cream
½ cup milk
Salt
Pepper

Paprika
½ teaspoon Worcestershire sauce
1 teaspoon onion, grated
1 (7½ oz.) can crab meat
1 (8 oz.) can lobster
½ cup dry sherry
Snipped parsley

In top of double boiler, combine soups, cream, milk, salt, pepper, paprika, and Worcestershire sauce. Beat with rotary beater. Stir in onion. Reserve a small amount of crab meat and lobster; add remainder to soup. Cover and cook over boiling water 45 minutes. Add sherry and heat. Add reserved crab and lobster to soup. Garnish with parsley. Serve with crusty French bread. Makes 4 servings.

CARIBBEAN AVOCADO SOUP

1 (11 oz.) can condensed Green
  Pea Soup
1 ripe avocado, peeled and cut up
1 (13 oz.) can evaporated milk
2 tablespoons dry sherry

2 tablespoons lemon juice
Lemon slices
Avocado slices
Fresh tomato, chopped

Combine soup, milk, and avocado in blender (reserve 4 slices for garnish.) Blend until smooth. Add sherry and lemon juice. Add more milk if too thick. Cover and chill well. Garnish with lemon and avocado slices and chopped tomato. Serve with cheese pastry. Makes 3 or 4 servings.

POTATO ALMOND SOUP

1 (10½ oz.) can condensed
  Cream of Potato Soup
1½ soup cans light cream
½ cup slivered toasted almonds

1 (14 oz.) can Chicken Broth
Dash pepper
Chopped chives or watercress

Combine soup and cream in blender. Reserve a few almonds for garnish; add remainder to blender. Blend until smooth. Pour into saucepan. Add broth and pepper. Heat slowly. Serve hot, garnished with chives or watercress and almonds. Makes 4 servings.

SPECIAL CHOICE SOUPS

Smörgasbord Soup will provide entertainment as well as nourishment for your guests or family. The variety of ingredients encourages them to use their imagination in creating a different and delicious soup each time they go back for more.

SMÖRGASBORD SOUP

2 quarts Brown Stock (p. 11)

8 slices Pickled Beets (p. 74)

10 green onions, chopped

6 frankfurters, cooked and sliced

6 stalks celery, cooked and sliced

6 carrots, cooked and sliced

1 bunch radishes, sliced

1 cup dairy sour cream

3 tablespoons caraway seeds

Croutons

Cheese popcorn

Grated Parmesan cheese

Heat stock. Place remaining ingredients in individual small bowls. Pour hot broth into tureen and arrange small bowls around tureen so that guests may help themselves to the tidbits and then ladle on the hot broth. Encourage guests to take a few ingredients each time and come back for a different combination later. For example, one could take a few beets, a ladle of soup, and then a topping of sour cream and chopped onion. You have a Borscht. Or you might take a few croutons, a ladle of soup, sprinkle with chopped onion and Parmesan cheese, and you have a good onion soup. Be sure to have a variety of crackers to serve along with soup. Makes 8 servings.

CHEESE SOUP

½ cup celery, chopped

½ cup carrots, chopped

¼ cup onion, minced

3 tablespoons butter

3 tablespoons flour

½ teaspoon salt

⅛ teaspoon paprika

3 cups milk

2 Chicken Bouillion cubes

1½ cups sharp cheese, grated

1½ cups grated sharp cheese

2 tablespoons snipped parsley

Cook celery and carrots in small amount of water until fork-tender. Drain, reserving ½ cup of the cooking water. Sauté onion in butter until transparent. Stir in flour, salt, and paprika. Cook over low heat, stirring until mixture is bubbly. Remove from heat. Gradually stir in milk. Heat to boiling, stirring constantly. Cook and stir 1 minute. Dissolve bouillon cubes in hot water; add to milk mixture. Add vegetables and reserved cooking water. Just before serving, heat well and add cheese. Heat just enough to melt cheese. Sprinkle with parsley. Serve with toasted French bread. Makes 4 servings.

CHINESE EGG FLOWER SOUP

¼ pound fresh mushrooms, sliced

2 tablespoons butter

½ cup julienne-style strips of pork

2 tablespoons oil

8 cups White Stock, Chicken (p. 12)

3 stalks celery, chopped

1 cup fresh spinach, chopped

2 eggs, beaten

Salt

Pepper

Sauté mushrooms in butter 5 minutes. Set aside. Sauté pork strips in oil about 6 minutes. Set aside. Heat stock in soup pot. Add celery, sautéed mushrooms and pork strips. Cook about 8 minutes. Just before serving, heat broth; add spinach and cook 5 minutes. Slowly add beaten eggs. Correct seasonings. Makes 6 to 8 servings.

EGG AND LEMON SOUP

6 cups White Stock, Chicken (p. 12)

⅓ cup uncooked regular rice

3 tablespoons lemon juice

4 eggs, slightly beaten

Salt

2 tablespoons mint leaves, finely cut

Bring stock to a boil and add rice. Reduce to simmer; cover and cook about 15 minutes or until rice is tender. Stir lemon juice and ¼ cup hot stock into eggs; return to pot, stirring constantly. Cook over low heat 5 minutes. Do not boil. Add salt to taste. Serve garnished with mint. Makes 6 servings.

SOUP WITH A FLAIR

2 tablespoons dried beef	12 flowerets fresh broccoli
1 tablespoon butter	2 tablespoons brandy
4 cups Cream of Chicken Stock (p. 13)	2 tablespoons parsley, chopped

Rinse dried beef in hot water. Chop and sauté in butter. Add Cream of Chicken Stock. Heat, stirring occasionally. Cook broccoli in small amount of boiling salted water until tender. Just before serving, add broccoli to soup. Bring the soup in a tureen and have a lighted candle nearby. Heat brandy in a small pan over the candle. When brandy is hot, tip into candle flame to ignite. Carefully add flaming brandy to soup and sprinkle with parsley. Makes 4 servings.

SOUP FLAMAND

1 pint fresh Brussel Sprouts	⅓ cup flour
3 cups White Stock, Chicken (p. 12)	3 cups milk
¼ cup butter	½ cup whipping cream
Salted whipped cream, if desired	

Cook sprouts in small amount boiling salted water 8 to 10 minutes or until tender; drain. Reserve about 12 sprouts. Purée remaining sprouts in blender or food mill, adding small amount of stock. Combine with remaining stock. Melt butter; stir in flour. Cook over low heat, stirring until mixture is smooth and bubbly. Remove from heat. Gradually stir in milk; heat to boiling, stirring constantly. Cook and stir 1 minute. Add sprout mixture and ½ cup whipping cream. Heat to serving temperature. Cut the reserved sprouts in half. Pour hot soup into tureen. Place sprouts around edge of tureen. Add a dollop of salted whipped cream in center, if desired. Makes 6 servings.

SAVOY CABBAGE SOUP

2 heads Savoy Cabbage, cut in
  large pieces
6 cups Brown Stock (p. 11)
6 tablespoons butter

3 tablespoons flour
4 potatoes, cooked and cubed
4 frankfurters, sliced
½ teaspoon salt
½ teaspoon pepper

Cook cabbage in stock. When tender, blend or purée cabbage and stock; set aside. Melt butter; blend in flour. Cook over low heat, stirring until mixture is smooth and bubbly. Remove from heat. Slowly stir in cabbage mixture; heat to boiling, stirring constantly. Cook 10 minutes. Add potatoes, frankfurters, and seasonings. Heat well. Makes 8 servings.

ACCOMPANIMENTS TO SOUPS

HOMEMADE NOODLES

2 cups flour

1 egg yolk

½ teaspoon salt

1½ teaspoons cooking oil

½ cup warm water

Place 1¾ cup flour in bowl. Make a well in the center and drop in egg yolk, salt, and water. Mix well with a fork and add more flour if necessary. Toss on board and knead until smooth. Cover with cloth and let rest 20 minutes. Roll into rectangles and cut as desired. This dough makes noodles, ravioli, and other shapes.

RYE BREAD SANDWICHES

¼ pound soft butter

½ teaspoon snipped parsley

¼ teaspoon snipped chives

¼ teaspoon tarragon

1 loaf snack rye bread,
thinly sliced

Mix butter and herbs. Spread bread with herb butter to make sandwiches. Wrap well and store several hours before serving.

Pirozhkis are Russian pastries that are usually served with a heavy soup. They can also be served with a meatless soup to balance the meal.

PIROZHKI

1 cup flour

1½ teaspoons baking powder

¾ teaspoon salt

½ cup shortening

1 egg

Ice water

Meat Filling (p. 53)

Mix dry ingredients and cut in shortening. Place egg in measuring cup; beat slightly with fork. Add enough ice water to egg to measure ½ cup;

mix with a fork. Add egg mixture to dry ingredients. Form into a ball; cover and let rest in refrigerator 30 minutes. On lightly floured surface, roll and cut into rounds. Spread with Meat Filling (below) and cover with another round. Bake at 375° until brown.

MEAT FILLING

1 cup cooked meat, chopped	**Salt**
½ teaspoon snipped parsley	**Pepper**
1 tablespoon onion, grated	**2 tablespoons gravy, if desired**

Mix meat, parsley, and onion; season to taste with salt and pepper. Stir in gravy if meat is dry. Mix well.

CORN BREAD

1 cup flour	**½ teaspoon salt**
1 cup yellow cornmeal	**2 eggs**
⅓ cup sugar	**3 tablespoons salad oil**
4 teaspoons baking powder	**1 cup milk**

Heat over to 400°. Mix dry ingredients together. Beat eggs; add oil and milk. Stir into dry mixture. Pour into greased pan, 11x7x1½ inches. Bake about 20 minutes, or until golden brown. When partially cool, cut bread in rectangles and split in half. Butter the cut sides and reheat just before serving.

PARMESAN CHIPS

1 loaf snack rye bread,	**½ cup grated Parmesan cheese**
** thinly sliced**	**¼ pound butter, melted**

Place bread slices on a cookie sheet overnight. They will dry and curl up. Paint both sides lightly with melted butter and dip in cheese. Bake in 350° oven until brown.(These keep well in a covered tin.)

CURRY ROLLS

16 slices white bread,	**½ teaspoon curry powder,**
** thinly sliced**	** or more if desired**
	¼ pound butter, melted

Remove crusts from bread slices. Mix curry powder with butter and spread lightly on bread. Roll each slice tightly and secure with a wooden pick. Place in a jelly roll pan and paint rolls with any remaining butter. Bake in 350° oven just before serving.

GARLIC CROUTONS

1 clove garlic, halved   1 loaf bread, preferably French
2 tablespoons salad or olive oil   2 tablespoons butter

Let garlic stand in oil overnight; remove garlic. Trim crusts from bread; cut in cubes. Place oil and butter in jelly roll pan and put in oven to melt butter. Add cubes of bread. Turn cubes about with spatula to coat evenly. Place in 350° oven and toast just until brown, turning once or twice.

PULLED BREAD

Break open an unsliced, day-old loaf of bread. Pull out chunks of the bread with your fingers or with a fork and toast in the oven.

CROUSTADES

½ pound soft butter   1 tablespoon tarragon
2 tablespoons parsley, chopped   1 clove garlic, pressed, if desired
2 tablespoons chives or green   Dash salt
     onion, chopped   Unsliced day-old bread

Mix butter, herbs, and salt. Cut bread in any size and shape desired. Spread with herb butter and heat in 350° oven. If toast is desired, continue heating until brown. This is much better than plain garlic bread. Any leftover butter may be used for vegetables.

SALADS

"Before man fitted stones to slings
Or wrote a song or ballad
He chewed up grass and weeds and things
But didn't know 'twas salad"

Unknown

CRISP, FRESH SALADS

Greens, the basic foundation of most salads, are among the most nutritious and refreshing of foods. Leafy lettuce, endive, cabbage, spinach, and many, many more can be used to create tempting, vitamin-rich salads.

To retain vitamins and keep greens fresh and crisp, wash and refrigerate them as soon as you get home from the store. And since greens start losing vitamin C as soon as they are torn, you should not tear them before you are ready to prepare the salad.

Wine should not be served with a salad that has a high vinegar or lemon content, nor should it be served with tomatoes. Chicken and fish salads are in reality cold entrées, and therefore wine may be served with them.

Parsley, chives, tarragon, and chervil are excellent herbs to use in salads, and basil can be used if there are tomatoes in the salad. White wine vinegar is best for making your own dressings.

Try a large, deep platter for serving the salad instead of the traditional bowl. It is easier to garnish and serve.

And, as with soups, let these recipes serve as guidelines to create your own nutritious salads!

CLASSIC SALAD DRESSINGS

There are many excellent prepared salad dressings on the shelf of your supermarket. When time permits, however, it's fun to make your own dressing, suited exactly to personal preferences in seasoning.

BASIC FRENCH DRESSING

⅓ cup white wine vinegar

¾ teaspoon salt

1 cup salad or olive oil

Freshly ground pepper

Put vinegar in bowl and add salt. Slowly add oil and beat continuously with a fork or wire whisk. Add pepper. Makes about 1⅓ cups.

RUSSIAN DRESSING

1 cup mayonnaise

1 cup dairy sour cream

½ cup chili sauce

2 tablespoons caviar, if desired

1 teaspoon prepared mustard

Snipped chives & parsley

Mix well; cover and chill. (This is also a very good dip for raw vegetables.) Makes about 2½ cups.

SAUCE VINAIGRETTE

⅓ cup white wine vinegar

1 teaspoon salt

1 green onion, chopped or

    1 tablespoon chives, snipped

2 sprigs parsley, minced

½ teaspoon tarragon

½ teaspoon dry mustard

1 cup salad or olive oil

Place vinegar, salt, onion, parsley, tarragon, and mustard in blender. Add ¼ cup oil and blend. Stop blender, add ¼ cup more oil, and blend. Repeat until all oil is used. (This dressing may be made in a glass pitcher and beaten by hand, but the blender makes a much thicker and tastier dressing.) Makes about 1⅓ cups.

SOUR CREAM DRESSING

1 cup dairy sour cream	1 tablespoon mayonnaise
2 tablespoons sugar	½ teaspoon salt
2 tablespoons wine vinegar	Dash white pepper

Mix well with a fork and let stand to mellow about 30 minutes. Makes about 1 cup.

CELERY SEED DRESSING

⅓ cup vinegar	1 teaspoon salt
¼ cup sugar or honey	1 teaspoon dry mustard
2 tablespoons apricot jam	1 cup salad oil
1 small onion, minced	2 tablespoons celery seed

1 tablespoon paprika, if desired

Place all ingredients except celery seeds and salad oil in blender and blend thoroughly. Add oil in three parts, blending after each addition. Add celery seeds last. Makes about 2 cups.

BASIC MAYONNAISE

2 tablespoons white wine vinegar	1 egg or 2 egg yolks
¾ teaspoon salt	1 cup salad oil
1 teaspoon dry mustard	

Place vinegar and salt in blender. Add mustard and egg. Add ¼ cup oil and blend. Add remainder of oil in 3 parts, blending after each addition. Makes about 1 cup.

BACON DRESSING

3 or 4 slices bacon, crumbled	1 tablespoon water
1 tablespoon sugar	Dash salt
3 tablespoons vinegar	

Sauté bacon until crisp and remove from pan. Add remaining ingredients to drippings. Reheat and taste. Reserve bacon bits to toss with greens if desired.

GREEN SALADS

GOURMET'S CHOICE

⅓ cup white wine vinegar

1 teaspoon salt

½ teaspoon dry mustard

3 sprigs fresh parsley

1 teaspoon fresh chives

5 sprigs watercress

3 sprigs fresh chervil

1 sprig fresh tarragon

1 head iceberg lettuce

1 head Boston lettuce

1 cup olive oil

Freshly ground pepper

Place vinegar, salt, and mustard in large glass bowl. Add herbs. Let stand at least 30 minutes. Have all greens washed, dried, and torn (not cut) in plastic bag in refrigerator. Have oil measured in a pitcher, and a pepper mill handy. Just before serving, place greens in bowl; pour on a little oil and toss lightly. Continue adding oil and tossing until all greens are coated. Now toss leaves with the vinegar and herbs. Sprinkle with freshly ground pepper. Makes 10 servings.

FRESH ENDIVE AND MUSHROOM SALAD

4 heads fresh endive

½ pound fresh mushrooms

2 bunches watercress

Sauce Vinaigrette (p. 61)

Few leaves Bibb lettuce, if desired

Clean and slice endive. Slice mushrooms lengthwise. Remove some of the stems from the watercress. Make Sauce Vinaigrette with lemon juice in place of vinegar. Toss greens and mushrooms with Sauce Vinaigrette. May be served on a leaf of Bibb lettuce, if desired. Makes 6 servings.

WILTED LETTUCE SALAD

Leaf lettuce

Bacon Dressing (p. 62)

Wash and dry leaf lettuce. Tear lettuce and place in large bowl. Toss reserved bacon bits from dressing with lettuce. Pour hot dressing over lettuce just before serving. This wilts the lettuce.

CAESAR SALAD

1 or 2 cloves garlic, halved	½ cup grated Parmesan cheese
½ cup olive oil	¼ teaspoon freshly ground pepper
2 heads Romaine lettuce	6 tablespoons olive oil
2 cups bread cubes	Juice of 1 lemon
¼ teaspoon dry mustard	2 raw eggs
½ teaspoon salt	

Place garlic cloves in ½ cup olive oil and let stand overnight. Have lettuce washed, dried, and chilled. Remove garlic from oil, sauté bread cubes in oil until light brown. Tear lettuce and place in very large bowl. Sprinkle with mustard, salt, and Parmesan cheese. Grind pepper over all. Drizzle with 6 tablespoons olive oil and lemon juice. Break in 1 egg at a time, tossing well and with great flair after each addition. Add croutons and serve. Makes 8 servings.

CHIFFONADE SALAD

Variety of greens	Garnish:
Celery, chopped, if desired	Pickled Beets (p. 74)
Hard-cooked eggs, separated	Watercress
Sauce Vinaigrette (p. 61)	Cherry tomatoes, cut in half
Snipped parsley and chives	

Have greens washed, dried and chilled. Break greens into salad bowl. Add celery. Chop egg whites and put yolks through a sieve. Add eggs to greens, reserving some for garnish. Toss gently with Sauce Vinaigrette. Place salad on large platter and garnish with pickled beets, watercress, and cherry tomatoes. Sprinkle with reserved eggs, parsley, and chives. Pass additional dressing. (This salad is excellent served with meat sandwiches, and preceded by a bowl of French Onion Soup (p. 21) is a complete meal.) Makes 8 servings.

CUCUMBER SALAD

1 or 2 cucumbers	1 tablespoon onion, grated
Salt	Shredded lettuce
½ cup mayonnaise	Snipped chives

Slice cucumbers thinly. Arrange some in a layer in glass dish and sprinkle with salt. Spread with mayonnaise and a little grated onion. Continue in layers, finishing with mayonnaise. Cover and chill 12 hours. Place on a bed of shredded lettuce and sprinkle with snipped chives. Makes 4 servings.

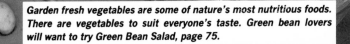

Garden fresh vegetables are some of nature's most nutritious foods. There are vegetables to suit everyone's taste. Green bean lovers will want to try Green Bean Salad, page 75.

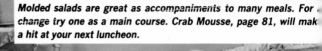
Molded salads are great as accompaniments to many meals. For a change try one as a main course. Crab Mousse, page 81, will make a hit at your next luncheon.

A combination of seafood and fresh tomatoes is the start of a tasty luncheon or supper dish. Seafood Salad, page 66, served with fresh tomato accordions is sure to please your family.

All these fresh vegetables can go into a soup or salad that will please your family. Try both of these fresh vegetable favorites, Farmer's Soup, page 24, and Tomato and Cucumber Salad, page 89.

CUCUMBER MOUSSE

2 cucumbers, pared

1 tablespoon lemon juice

1 teaspoon Worcestershire sauce

1 teaspoon salt

¼ teaspoon white pepper

¼ cup mayonnaise

1 envelope unflavored gelatin

2 tablespoons cold water

1 tablespoon hot water

½ cup cream

Green food coloring, if desired

Garnish:

  Cucumber

  Watercress

Sauce Vinaigrette (p. 61)

Mayonnaise with chives and parsley

Cut cucumbers in half and scoop out seeds. Blanch for 5 minutes in boiling water to which lemon juice has been added. Drain and put in blender and blend 7 seconds. Cool and add Worcestershire sauce, salt, pepper, and mayonnaise. Soak gelatin in cold water and add hot water. Dissolve. Add to cucumber mixture. Whip cream and add. A few drops of green food coloring may be added, if desired. Put in oiled mold. To serve, unmold and garnish with watercress and slices of cucumber marinated in Sauce Vinaigrette. Pass mayonnaise to which chives and parsley have been added. Serve with cheese bread sticks. Makes 6 servings.

CRAB LOUIS

Shredded lettuce

Cooked crab meat

Hard-cooked eggs, separated

Sauce Louis (below)

Cover scallop shells or salad plates with shredded lettuce. Arrange cooked crab meat on lettuce and sprinkle chopped egg whites around edge. Add sieved yolks to center. Serve with Sauce Louis and Poppy Seed Sticks (p. 91).

SAUCE LOUIS

½ cup mayonnaise, or

  Basic Mayonnaise (p. 62)

½ cup chili sauce

2 tablespoons pickle relish

¼ cup celery, chopped

1 teaspoon Worcestershire sauce

Salt

Mix all ingredients together. Salt to taste. Cover and chill. Makes about 1 cup.

SEAFOOD SALAD

Your choice of seafood:
  Shrimp
  Lobster
  Crab
  Salmon

Your choice of vegetables:
  Cauliflower

Carrots
Green beans
Lima beans
Beets
Sauce Vinaigrette (p. 61)
Shredded lettuce
Mayonnaise Verte (below)

Cook your choice of seafood and vegetables. Drain. Place seafood and vegetables in separate shallow dishes; pour on Sauce Vinaigrette. Cover and marinate in refrigerator several hours or overnight, turning seafood and vegetables occasionally. Just before serving, toss shredded lettuce with Sauce Vinaigrette and arrange as a border on platter. Remove seafood and vegetables with a slotted spoon and arrange in center of platter. Drizzle Sauce Vinaigrette over all. Serve with Mayonnaise Verte.

MAYONNAISE VERTE

1 recipe Basic Mayonnaise (p. 62)
2 tablespoons chives, snipped
2 tablespoons parsley, snipped
2 tablespoons watercress, snipped
1 tablespoon tarragon

Prepare Basic Mayonnaise as directed, *except* substitute lemon juice for vinegar and add above herbs with mustard and egg. Cover and chill to blend flavors. (Mayonnaise Verte goes well with seafood and fish of all kinds.) Makes about 1 cup. *Note:* For a quick version, mix above herbs with 1 cup commercial mayonnaise; cover and chill to blend flavors.

SPRINGTIME SALAD

8 radishes, sliced
¼ pound fresh green beans, cooked and cooled
¼ pound fresh green peas, cooked and cooled
1 cucumber, sliced

½ cup Sauce Vinaigrette (p. 61)
4 hard-cooked eggs, cut in wedges
Salt
12 cherry tomatoes
Mayonnaise
Snipped parsley and chives

Combine radishes, green beans, peas, and cucumbers in salad bowl. Pour Sauce Vinaigrette over vegetables; cover and marinate in refrigerator 30 minutes or longer. Just before serving, pour off excess dressing. Garnish with salted cherry tomatoes and egg wedges. Cover with a very thin layer of mayonnaise and sprinkle with snipped parsley and chives. Makes 6 servings.

CABBAGE AND SPINACH SALADS

COLESLAW

1 cup sugar

2 tablespoons water

⅓ cup vinegar

Celery seed, if desired

Dash of salt

½ medium cabbage, shredded

(green or red cabbage, or half

of each)

Place sugar, water, and vinegar in saucepan; stir to mix. Heat dressing, stirring until sugar dissolves. Remove from heat and add celery seed. Salt to taste. While still warm, pour dressing over shredded cabbage and let stand about 30 minutes. Makes 4 servings.

CREAMY COLESLAW

½ medium cabbage, shredded

1 recipe Sweet-Sour

Dressing (below)

Green pepper, chopped

Pimiento, chopped

¼ cup mayonnaise

¼ cup whipped cream

Dash salt

Soak shredded cabbage in ice water 30 minutes. Drain. Meanwhile prepare Sweet-Sour Dressing. Pour over shredded cabbage. Let stand 30 minutes. Pour off excess dressing. Add green pepper and pimiento; toss lightly. Mix mayonnaise, whipped cream, and salt. Pour over cabbage. Makes 6 servings.

SWEET-SOUR DRESSING

⅓ cup white wine vinegar

¼ cup sugar

½ teaspoon salt

White pepper to taste

Paprika to taste

Combine vinegar, sugar, salt, white pepper, and paprika in saucepan. Heat, stirring until sugar dissolves. Makes about ½ cup.

SHRIMP AND AVOCADO ON CREAM SLAW

½ medium cabbage, shredded
1 recipe Sweet-Sour
  Dressing (p. 67)
½ cup dairy sour cream

3 avocados, peeled and halved
Cooked shrimp
Tangy Dressing (below)

Soak shredded cabbage in ice water 30 minutes. Meanwhile prepare
Sweet-Sour Dressing; cool. Slowly stir into sour cream. Drain cabbage
and dry. Toss with dressing. Arrange a bed of slaw on salad plates.
Place an avocado half, rounded side up, on each plate; surround with
shrimp. Pass Tangy Dressing. (This is a fine entrée for a luncheon.)
Makes 6 servings.

TANGY DRESSING

1 cup mayonnaise
¼ cup catsup
1 tablespoon vinegar
½ teaspoon salt

1 tablespoon onion, grated
2 teaspoons Worcestershire sauce
1 tablespoon prepared horseradish

Mix well; cover and chill.

SALAD BOUQUET

½ cup sugar
1 teaspoon dry mustard
3 eggs, beaten
½ cup vinegar
Dash cayenne pepper
Heavy cream
½ cabbage, shredded

Garnish:
  Cucumber sticks
  Carrots
  Celery with leaves
  Green onions with tops
  Radishes

Mix sugar, dry mustard, eggs, vinegar, and pepper; cook in top of double boiler until thick. Cook and thin with cream to desired thickness.
Mix shredded cabbage with dressing. Place in bowl. Just before serving, garnish with raw vegetables on picks. The dressing in the salad will
serve as a dip. Tops of celery and green onions act as leaves for the
bouquet. Makes 6 servings.

GOURMET SPINACH SALAD

1 package fresh spinach	1 teaspoon lemon juice
2 hard-cooked eggs, chopped	Cherry tomatoes
2 tablespoons salad oil	1 recipe Tomato-Herb Dressing (below)

Wash and tear spinach, discarding stems. Dry and chill. Toss with oil and lemon juice. Add eggs and tomatoes. Pass Tomato-Herb Dressing. Makes 6 servings.

TOMATO-HERB DRESSING

1 egg	1 tablespoon sugar
¼ teaspoon mustard	½ teaspoon basil
Dash white pepper	1 teaspoon Worcestershire sauce
1 tablespoon paprika	1 cup salad oil
2 teaspoons salt	⅓ cup white wine vinegar
½ (6 oz.) can tomato paste	½ cup warm water

Place all but last 3 ingredients in blender and blend. Add oil and vinegar alternately, blending in between. Add water and blend. Cool. Makes about 2 cups.

SPINACH AND CUCUMBER SALAD

1 package fresh spinach	5 pitted ripe olives, sliced
2 cucumbers	5 pimiento-stuffed green olives,
1 cup celery, sliced	sliced
½ cup parsley, snipped	¼ cup pine nuts, if desired
Sauce Vinaigrette (p. 61)	Oregano

Wash and tear spinach, discarding stems. Dry and chill. Pare cucumber; quarter and remove seeds. Chop cucumbers. Add cucumber, celery, and parsley to spinach. Toss lightly with Sauce Vinaigrette. Add olives and pine nuts. Sprinkle with oregano. Pass additional Sauce Vinaigrette. Makes 6 servings.

SPINACH SALAD WITH WATERCRESS DRESSING

1 head lettuce	**Sauce Vinaigrette (p. 61)**
1 package fresh spinach	**Watercress**
Radishes, sliced	**3 tablespoons light cream**

Wash and shred lettuce and spinach; dry well. Add sliced radishes and chill. Prepare Sauce Vinaigrette as directed, *except* substitute watercress for parsley, using slightly more watercress. Just before serving, add the cream and toss lightly with greens. Makes 6 servings.

HOT SPINACH LETTUCE BOWL

½ head lettuce	**1 (4 oz.) can sliced mushrooms**
1 package fresh spinach	**(with liquid)**
2 tablespoons butter	**2 tablespoons lemon juice**
1 tablespoon cornstarch	**2 teaspoons sugar**
Dash salt	

Wash and tear lettuce and spinach, discarding spinach stems. Dry and chill. Melt butter and blend in cornstarch. Stir in mushrooms, including liquid. Cook, stirring constantly, until mixture thickens and boils; cook and stir 1 minute. Add lemon juice, sugar, and salt. Add greens and toss until slightly wilted. Serve immediately. Makes 6 servings.

SAUERKRAUT SALAD

1 pint sauerkraut	**2 apples, peeled and chopped**
3 tablespoons oil	**2 carrots, grated**
2 tablespoons onion, grated	**2 to 3 tablespoons vinegar**
Salt, if needed	

Wash sauerkraut and drain. Chop and mix with oil, onion, and salt. Add apples and carrots. Moisten with vinegar. Chill. Serve with Rye Bread Sandwiches (p. 52). Makes 6 servings.

VEGETABLE SALADS

CAULIFLOWER SALAD

1 whole head cauliflower

Fresh spinach or Boston lettuce

1 recipe Olive-Caper

Dressing (below)

Cook cauliflower in boiling salted water 10 to 12 minutes. Drain. Place in bowl with flower side up. Weight with a plate and heavy object. After 15 minutes, drain excess water from cauliflower. Chill for 2 hours. Wash and tear spinach, discarding stems. Dry and chill. Place cauliflower on platter; surround with torn spinach or Boston lettuce. Pour Olive-Caper Dressing over salad. Pass additional dressing. Makes 6 servings.

OLIVE-CAPER DRESSING

½ cup lemon juice

2 tablespoons capers, chopped

2 tablespoons parsley, snipped

2 tablespoons watercress, cut up

¼ cup pimiento-stuffed olives, chopped

1 teaspoon salt

Dash cayenne pepper

1 cup oil (mixture or olive and salad oils)

Place all ingredients except oil in blender. Add oil in three parts, blending after each addition. (This can be done by hand with rotary or electric beater, but a better emulsion is formed with a blender.) Makes about 2 cups.

GUACAMOLE SALAD

Shredded lettuce

5 slices bacon, fried crisp

2 tablespoons almonds, chopped

3 ripe avocados

3 tablespoons lemon juice

1 tablespoon Worcestershire sauce

¼ teaspoon salt

1 teaspoon curry powder

Dash cayenne pepper

Dash sugar

Dash garlic powder

Shred lettuce and fry bacon. Chop almonds; set aside. Just before serving, peel and pit avocados; chop. Quickly stir in remaining ingredients.

Stir in chopped almonds. Spoon over shredded lettuce. Crumble bacon over top. Pass toasted Corn Bread (p. 53). Makes 6 servings.

AVOCADO MAGNIFIQUE

4 avocados, not too ripe   **Dressing Magnifique (below)**

Cut avocados in half. Remove seeds and fill center with dressing. Just before serving, broil about 4 minutes. Makes 8 servings.

DRESSING MAGNIFIQUE

2 sprigs parsley	**½ (6 oz.) can tomato paste**
1 stalk celery	**2 tablespoons brown sugar**
1 green onion	**¼ cup walnuts**
1 clove garlic, pressed	**1 teaspoon dry mustard**
1 teaspoon salt	**1 cup oil**
⅓ cup vinegar	**Pepper to taste**
¼ cup orange juice	

Place vegetables, salt, and vinegar in blender. Let stand 10 minutes, then blend. Add orange juice, tomato paste, sugar, and nuts. Blend again. Add mustard and oil in three parts, blending after each addition. Correct seasoning. This is a most unusual salad, but the combination of hot dressing and cool avocado is wonderful.

ASPARAGUS VINAIGRETTE

1 bunch fresh asparagus	**Shredded lettuce**
Sauce Vinaigrette (p. 61) or	**Snipped parsley**
bottled herb French dressing	**1 hard-cooked egg, separated**

Break off ends of asparagus and wash. Cook in small amount boiling salted water just until fork-tender. Drain and cool. Place in shallow dish; drizzle with Sauce Vinaigrette or bottled dressing. Cover and marinate in refrigerator several hours or overnight. Arrange asparagus on bed of shredded lettuce on individual salad plates. Mix snipped parsley, chopped egg white and sieved egg yolk; sprinkle over asparagus. (This is a fine first course for a sit-down dinner.) Makes 4 servings.

TOMATO SALAD

1 Spanish onion

2 or 3 tomatoes, preferably
Beefsteak

Sugar

Salt and pepper

Snipped chives

Basil

Celery seed

Sauce Vinaigrette (p. 61) or
bottled oil & vinegar dressing

Shredded lettuce

Slice onion and separate into rings. Place in a bowl. Peel tomatoes; cut into thick slices. Cover onion with tomato slices and sprinkle with sugar, salt, pepper, chives, basil, and celery seed. Drizzle with a small amount Sauce Vinaigrette. Cover and chill. Arrange chilled lettuce on individual salad plates. Transfer tomato and onion slices to plates or pass the bowl, allowing guests to help themselves. Pass dressing. Makes 6 servings.

CHILLED TOMATO SALAD

3 cups tomatoes, cooked

3 tablespoons sugar

2 teaspoons salt

Dash pepper

2 tablespoons onion juice

2 tablespoons unflavored gelatin

⅓ cup cold water

½ cup cucumbers, chopped

½ cup celery, chopped

½ cup green pepper, chopped

½ cup cream

1 cup mayonnaise

1 tablespoon horseradish, if desired

Lettuce

Pimiento

Black olives

Cook tomatoes with sugar, salt, pepper, and onion for 10 minutes. Soak gelatin in cold water and dissolve in hot tomato mixture. Cool and add vegetables. Whip cream and blend with mayonnaise and horseradish. Blend into tomato mixture. Pour into oiled molds and set. Unmold on lettuce and garnish with pimiento and black olives. Makes 6 servings.

CHERRY TOMATO SALAD

1 basket or 2 cups cherry
tomatoes

1 bunch watercress

½ cup dairy sour cream

¼ cup mayonnaise

Salt

Pepper

1 tablespoon lemon juice

1 tablespoon horseradish

1 tablespoon chives

Pour boiling water over the tomatoes. Let set 2 minutes, then peel. Place the watercress in salad bowl and add the tomatoes carefully.

Chill. Mix remainder of ingredients and just before serving, pour over the tomatoes. Serve at once. Makes 6 servings.

DINNER SALAD

4 medium tomatoes, peeled
  and sliced

1 medium cucumber, pared and
  sliced

4 ounces Roquefort or bleu cheese,
  if desired

2 bunches watercress

Sauce Vinaigrette (p. 61) or
  bottled herb French dressing

Alternate slices of tomato and cucumber on salad plates. Sprinkle with bits of cheese and garnish with watercress. Pass Sauce Vinaigrette. Makes 6 servings.

PICKLED BEETS

½ cup water

¼ cup vinegar

1 stick cinnamon

8 cloves

¼ teaspoon salt

¼ cup sugar

10 fresh beets, cooked, peeled
  and sliced

Heat water with seasonings and sugar. Add beets and simmer 8 minutes. Cover and chill 24 hours.

PICKLED BEET SALAD

1 recipe Pickled Beets (above),
  cut julienne-style

6 green onions, chopped

Sauce Vinaigrette (p. 61) or
  bottled oil & vinegar dressing

¼ teaspoon horseradish, or
  to taste

Boston lettuce

1 hard-cooked egg, chopped

Combine beets with chopped green onions. Toss gently to coat with Sauce Vinaigrette, to which a little horseradish has been added. Serve on a leaf of Boston lettuce and garnish with chopped egg. Makes 6 servings.

GARDEN SALAD

1 pound fresh green peas

½ cup celery, chopped

½ cup Sauce Vinaigrette (p. 61) or
  bottled garlic French dressing

½ head lettuce, shredded

2 hard-cooked eggs, chopped

Cook peas in boiling salted water 8 to 10 minutes or until tender. Drain; cool. Add chopped celery; stir in Sauce Vinaigrette. Cover and marinate in refrigerator several hours or overnight. Spoon on a bed of shredded lettuce and garnish with chopped egg. Makes 6 servings.

GREEN BEAN SALAD

2 cups green beans, cooked (see
   instructions below)

2 hard-cooked eggs

½ cup cucumber, diced

2 tablespoons onions , chopped

2 tablespoons sweet pickles,
   chopped

½ teaspoon salt

¼ teaspoon paprika

⅓ cup Basic Mayonnaise (p. 62)

Mix all ingredients well and chill. Makes 6 servings.

How to cook green beans for a salad: Wash and remove ends of fresh green beans. Into a large kettle of boiling water drop a handful of beans at a time, being careful to keep the water boiling. Boil about 8 minutes. Have a cup of cold water handy and drop a bean in to test for tenderness. Cook them "al dente" (to the tooth). Add salt. Drain and run cold water over beans and place in bowl with a tray of ice cubes. Chill fast. Marinate in Sauce Vinaigrette (p. 61) if recipe calls for it. Always cook beans whole and do not add salt until the end.

SALAD LOUIS

1 cucumber, partially pared

¼ cup Basic French Dressing (p. 61)
   or bottled French desssing

1 cup Basic Mayonnaise (p. 62)

¼ cup dairy sour cream

½ teaspoon snipped chives

1 teaspoon snipped parsley

½ teaspoon tarragon

6 medium whole tomatoes

Shredded lettuce

Celery sticks

Radishes

Cut cucumber in chunks, combine with French dressing in blender, and blend. Add mayonnaise, sour cream, chives, parsley, and tarragon. Blend 2 seconds. Scoop out most of the inside of the tomatoes and turn upside down to drain. Place upright on bed of shredded lettuce and fill with cucumber dressing. (Sliced tomatoes may be used instead of whole tomatoes if desired.) Serve with a few celery sticks and some radishes at the side for dipping in dressing. Makes 6 servings.

EGGPLANT SALAD

1 eggplant	1 clove garlic, pressed
1 onion, minced	2 tablespoons vinegar
1 tomato	Lettuce
1 teaspoon sugar	Cherry tomatoes, halved
Salt	Cauliflower flowerets, cooked
Pepper	Sauce Vinaigrette (p. 61) or
¼ teaspoon basil	bottled Italian dressing

Wrap eggplant in foil and bake until tender, approximately 30 minutes. Cool. Pare and chop fine. Chop onion and tomato, add sugar, salt, pepper, basil, garlic, and vinegar. Add mixture to chopped eggplant and chop again until very fine. Taste for seasoning. Cover and chill well. Serve on bed of lettuce on individual salad plates. Marinate cherry tomatoes and cauliflower flowerets in Sauce Vinaigrette or bottled dressing, and garnish salad by arranging them alternately in a circle around eggplant. Makes 6 servings.

FRUIT SALADS

EDEN'S SALAD

Shredded lettuce

Basic French Dressing (p. 61) or
  bottled French dressing

Fresh fruit:
  Melon balls
  Pineapple chunks
  Grapes

Apple wedges

Avocado sprinkled with
  pomegranate seeds

Celery Seed Dressing (p. 62)

Sour Cream Dressing (p. 62)

Chutney Dressing (p. 81)

Toss lettuce with French dressing. Arrange on individual salad plates. Arrange fruit on lettuce and pass Celery Seed, Sour Cream and Chutney Dressings.

PINEAPPLE AND AVOCADO SALAD

2 cups fresh pineapple chunks

1 avocado, peeled and cubed

Lemon juice

1 teaspoon green ginger, grated
  (candied ginger may be
  substituted)

⅓ cup currant jelly

1 teaspoon paprika

1 cup mayonnaise

1 head Boston lettuce

Toss pineapple and avocado together; sprinkle with lemon juice and ginger. Cover tightly and let stand 1 hour. With fork, break jelly into small bits. Add jelly with paprika to mayonnaise and toss this with fruit. Chill. Serve on leaves of Boston lettuce. Makes 6 servings.

SUNBURST SALAD

1 grapefruit

1 large orange

4 heads Bibb lettuce

Celery Seed Dressing (p. 62)

Pare and cut fruit in segments. Flatten each Bibb lettuce leaf; arrange fruit in center in a sunburst. Make Celery Seed Dressing, *except* substitute poppy seed for celery seed. Pass dressing. Makes 4 servings.

SUMMER SALAD

12 Honeydew melon balls

12 cantaloupe balls

12 fresh pineapple chunks

12 Bing cherries, or strawberries

12 watermelon cubes

½ fresh nectarine

Lemon juice

Fine sugar

Leaf lettuce, edges dipped

In paprika

Honey French Dressing (below)

Marinate fruit in lemon juice. Sprinkle with fine sugar. Place fruit on lettuce leaves. Pass Honey French Dressing. Makes 6 servings.

HONEY FRENCH DRESSING

⅓ cup lemon juice

¾ teaspoon salt

1 tablespoon sugar

¼ cup honey

1 cup salad oil

Mix lemon juice and salt in blender. Add sugar and honey. Slowly add oil, blending continuously.

SPICED PEACHES

3 or 4 fresh peaches, sliced

½ cup water

¼ cup vinegar

½ cup sugar

2 sticks cinnamon

8 whole cloves

1 star anns, if desired

Make a syrup of water, vinegar, sugar, and spices. Add fruit and simmer 8 minutes. Cover and chill overnight. Fruits such as apricots, figs, pineapple, or mandarines may also be used. Makes 4 servings.

SURPRISE SALAD

1 head lettuce

French Dressing (p. 61) or
    bottled French dressing

¼ pound baked ham, cubed

¼ pound white chicken, cubed

16 melon balls

20 pineapple chunks

1 stalk celery, cut up

Sour Cream Dressing (p. 62)

Celery Seed Dressing (p. 62)

Tear lettuce and place in salad bowl. Toss with French dressing. Just before serving, add ham, chicken, melon balls, pineapple, and celery. Toss lightly. Pass Sour Cream and Celery Seed Dressings. Makes 6 servings.

APPETIZER SALAD

1 envelope unflavored gelatin	2 tablespoons lemon juice
¼ cup cold water	½ teaspoon Worcestershire sauce
1 tablespoon sugar	¼ cup celery, chopped
½ teaspoon salt	½ cup radishes, sliced, plus
3 whole cloves	16 radishes for garnish
1 piece stick cinnamon	8 small cucumber slices
2 cups tomato juice	2 tablespoons green onion, chopped

Soften gelatin in cold water. Add sugar, salt, and spices to 1 cup of tomato juice. Simmer 5 minutes and strain. Add gelatin, lemon
juice and remaining tomato juice. Add Worcestershire sauce and chill
until slightly thickened but not set. Stir in celery, radishes, and green
onion. Pour into 6 to 8 parfait glasses; chill until firm. Decorate the
top of each glass with a kabob made of 2 radishes and 1 cucumber
slice inserted into set gelatin. Makes 6 to 8 servings.

FRESH PINEAPPLE SALAD

2 large (or 4 small) pineapples	16 strawberries
Orange liqueur and fine sugar	Celery Seed Dressing (p. 62)
16 melon balls	Sprigs of mint
Lemon juice and fine sugar	

Cut pineapples in halves or quarters, leaving tops on, and cut out the
fruit. Reserve shells. Toss pineapple fruit with fine sugar and orange li-
queur. Cover and chill several hours. Sprinkle melon balls with lemon
juice and fine sugar. Hull the strawberries. Just before serving, combine fruit and toss lightly with Celery Seed Dressing. Arrange in
pineapple shells and garnish with sprigs of mint. Makes 8 servings.
Serve with Poppy Seed Sticks (p. 91).

MAIN COURSE SALADS

RUSSIAN SALAD

1 head Iceberg lettuce	2 tomatoes, cut in wedges
1 head Romaine lettuce	4 hard-cooked eggs, cut in wedges
Sauce Vinaigrette (p. 61)	3-ounces caviar
12 large shrimp, cooked	6 Pickled Beet slices (p. 74)
1 cucumber, peeled and sliced	Russian Dressing (p. 61)

Wash, dry, and tear lettuce. Chill. Toss lightly with Sauce Vinaigrette. Serve in large salad bowl or in individual ones. Garnish with shrimp, cucumber, tomato, eggs with caviar, and beets. Pass Russian Dressing. Makes 6 servings.

CHICKEN SALAD

1 stalk celery	Light cream, if desired
1 onion	Celery, cut up
2 sprigs parsley	Boston lettuce
1 carrot	Salted almonds
Salt	Avocado fingers
Pepper	Tomatoes, cut in wedges
3 quarts water	Ripe olives
3-to-4 pound chicken	Chutney Dressing (p. 81)
Mayonnaise	Sour Cream Dressing (p. 62)

Place celery stalk, onion, parsley, carrot, salt, and pepper in water; bring to a boil. Drop prepared chicken in boiling water, whole if possible. Simmer until tender and cool slightly. (Save broth for soups.) Remove meat from bones. Thin mayonnaise with a little cream, if desired; add celery and chicken meat. (The meat is still a little warm.) Mix carefully and chill. This may be done the day before. To serve, line a plate or shallow bowl with avocado, tomato, and olives. Pass Chutney Dressing and Sour Cream Dressing. This is chicken salad at its finest. Makes 6 servings.

CHUTNEY DRESSING

Mayonnaise to taste   **¼ cup chutney**

Mix well and chill before serving.

CRAB MOUSSE

1½ envelopes unflavored gelatin	**1 tablespoon parsley, chopped**
¼ cup cold water	**1 tablespoon chives, chopped**
2 tablespoons lime	**1 tablespoon prepared mustard**
Salt	**2 (7½ oz.) cans crab meat**
Pepper	**Lemon and lime slices**
2 tablespoons lemon	**¼ cup Gloucester Sauce (below)**

Soak gelatin in cold water. Dissolve in cold water in the top of a double boiler, or over hot water. Let cool slightly and add remaining ingredients. Pour into oiled mold and let set. Unmold and garnish with lemon and lime slices; serve with Gloucester Sauce on the side. Served with watercress sandwiches, this makes a wonderful summer lunch. Makes 8 servings.

GLOUCESTER SAUCE

1 cup mayonnaise	**2 tablespoons lemon juice**
¼ cup sour cream	**¼ teaspoon lemon rind**
	½ teaspoon Worcestershire sauce

Blend ingredients together.

GREEK SALAD

2 heads Boston lettuce	**3 small tomatoes, sliced**
1 cucumber, sliced	**12 cubes Feta cheese**
1 green pepper, cut up	**12 ripe olives (Greek if possible)**
8 radishes, sliced	**12 walnut halves**
6 green onions, sliced	**5 anchovies**
	Classic Herb Dressing (p. 82)

Wash and dry lettuce; separate leaves. Make a layer of lettuce leaves and place on them slices of cucumber, green pepper, radishes, green onions, and tomatoes. Repeat layers, making each smaller in pyramid fashion, until all vegetables are used. Now tuck in cheese, olives, and walnuts. Garnish with anchovies. Make Classic Herb Dressing and pour over top of salad. The dressing will trickle down and marinate salad. Pass additional dressing. Serve with crusty Greek bread. This is one of the world's greatest salads. Makes 6 servings.

CLASSIC HERB DRESSING

½ cup vinegar

1 teaspoon salt

½ teaspoon oregano

¼ teaspoon freshly ground pepper

1 cup olive oil

2 tablespoons lemon juice

Place vinegar in pitcher or bowl and add salt, oregano, and pepper. Beat with fork or wire whisk, gradually adding the olive oil. Add lemon juice.

SALAD NICOISE

1 head Boston lettuce

8 small potatoes, cooked

1 pound fresh green beans, cooked and drained

3 small tomatoes, cut in wedges

1 can anchovies

1 recipe Sauce Vinaigrette (p. 61)

1 (7½ oz.) can white tuna (albacore)

12 ripe olives

4 hard-cooked eggs

Wash and dry lettuce; chill. Separate leaves and place on salad platter. Combine potatoes, beans, tomatoes, and Sauce Vinaigrette. Cover and chill several hours. Arrange the tuna and the vegetables in clusters on lettuce and garnish with olives and eggs. Place anchovies on a small plate beside the salad.(It is best not to put anchovies in a salad, as their flavor is so penetrating, and some people do not like them.) Makes 6 servings.

GREEN GODDESS SALAD

8 anchovy filets

2 green onions (with tops)

4 sprigs parsley

½ teaspoon tarragon

1 teaspoon chives

2 tablespoons white wine vinegar

2 cups mayonnaise

2 heads Boston lettuce, torn up

Place anchovies, green onions, parsley, tarragon, chives, and vinegar in blender; blend until smooth. Add mayonnaise. Blend only to mix. Toss dressing with Boston lettuce. Served with a meat sandwich, this makes an excellent supper. Makes 4 servings.

IMPERIAL SALAD

½ cup Roquefort or bleu cheese

3 tablespoons dairy sour cream

½ teaspoon Dijon mustard

¼ teaspoon Worcestershire sauce

Salt

6 tablespoons oil (mixture of olive oil and salad oil)

Pepper

2 tablespoons white wine vinegar

Assorted lettuces

Tomato and avocado slices

Artichoke hearts

Hard-cooked eggs

Croutons

Combine cheese, sour cream, mustard, Worcestershire sauce, salt, pepper, vinegar, and oil. Serve on remaining ingredients. This salad must be rolled, carefully turning the top under with spoon and fork, not tossed. Add croutons just before serving. Makes 6 servings.

SALAD CHEVAL BLEU

¼ cup lemon juice

¼ cup white wine vinegar

1 teaspoon salt

1 teaspoon Dijon mustard

¾ cup salad oil

¼ cup olive oil

2 anchovies

¼ cup grated Parmesan cheese

1 egg

Freshly ground pepper

Assorted greens

Place lemon juice, vinegar, and salt in blender. Add mustard and ¼ cup salad oil. Blend 7 seconds and add the olive oil. Blend. Add anchovies and another ¼ cup salad oil and blend. Add remaining salad oil and blend. Add Parmesan cheese, egg, and pepper; blend. Toss with assorted greens and serve with garlic toast. Makes 6 servings.

BIG SALAD

1 (16 oz.) can garbanzos (chick-peas)

Sauce Vinaigrette (p. 61)

3 heads assorted lettuce

½ pound salami, cut in julienne strips

10 radishes, sliced

8 green onions, sliced

Green pepper, sliced

6 stalks celery, sliced

Snipped parsley

12 cherry tomatoes

Drain and wash garbanzos and marinate in Sauce Vinaigrette 2 hours or longer. Wash, dry, tear lettuce and place in plastic bag; chill.

Just before serving, toss greens with Sauce Vinaigrette and add meat, vegetables, and parsley. Toss lightly and garnish with cherry tomatoes. Serve this as a main course with hot French bread. Makes 10 servings.

HOT POTATO SALAD

18 medium-size red potatoes	½ teaspoon pepper
½ pound bacon	½ cup water
⅓ cup vinegar	2 tablespoons green onions,
½ cup sugar	chopped
2 teaspoons salt	1 tablespoon parsley, chopped

2 hard-cooked eggs

Boil potatoes until fork-tender. Peel and slice in bowl. Cover with cloth to keep warm. Dice bacon and fry until crisp. Remove. Add vinegar, sugar, salt, pepper, and water to the drippings to make a dressing, and bring to a boil. Sprinkle onions and parsley over potatoes. Pour dressing over all. Garnish with chopped egg and bacon bits. Makes 6 servings.

POTATO SALAD WITH GARNISH

3 pounds red potatoes	¼ cup chives, chopped
¼ cup Basic French Dressing	Hard-cooked eggs, sliced
(p. 61)	Tomato wedges
Buttermilk for thinning	Cucumber slices
Fresh Basic Mayonnaise (p. 62)	Radishes
Parsley, chopped	Green onions

Celery curls

Boil potatoes in jackets until fork-tender. Drop in ice water to stop cooking. Peel and slice. Pour the French Dressing over the potatoes while they are still warm. Add a little buttermilk to mayonnaise to thin slightly and toss gently. Chill well in round bowl. When ready to serve, unmold on large round platter. Sprinkle with parsley, chives and garnish with slices of egg. Place tomato wedges, cucumber slices, radishes, green onions, and celery curls around salad. This salad can be made the day before, but do not garnish until ready to serve. Makes 6 servings.

SALAD EMELINE

3 heads assorted lettuce
Sauce Vinaigrette (p. 61) or
   bottled herb French dressing
Bibb or leaf lettuce for garnish
½ pound white meat of turkey or
   chicken, shredded

Baked ham, julienne-style
Cucumber, sliced
Tomato, cut in wedges
Hard-cooked egg, quartered

Wash, dry, and tear lettuce in salad bowl; toss with Sauce Vinaigrette. Line sides of bowl with Bibb or leaf lettuce leaves. Garnish lavishly with turkey or chicken and baked ham, cucumber, tomato, and hard-cooked egg. Pass Emeline Dressing (below) with salad. Serve with toasted hard rolls. A great salad for a summer lunch. Makes 8 servings.

EMELINE DRESSING

1 cucumber
½ cup Sauce Vinaigrette (p. 61) or
   bottled herb French dressing
1 cup mayonnaise

1 teaspoon Dijon mustard
½ teaspoon tarragon
½ cup sour cream
Parsley

Partially pare cucumber, cut it up, and place in blender. Add Sauce Vinaigrette and blend. Add mayonnaise, mustard, tarragon, and sour cream. Blend 2 seconds. Add freshly chopped parsley.

LEBANESE SALAD

Lettuce leaves
Cucumber, sliced
Small tomatoes, sliced
Green onions, chopped

Snipped parsley
Basic French Dressing (p. 61) or
   bottled French dressing

Line platter with lettuce leaves. Alternate slices of cucumber and slices of tomatoes. Sprinkle with chopped green onions and parsley. Prepare Basic French Dressing *except* substitute lemon juice for vinegar. Serve with lamb shish kabobs and hot French bread.

HORS D'OEUVRES

These little salads should be served in small dishes called "raviers." A choice of six to twelve are usually served. They are neatly arranged and garnished simply. Here is a partial list with instructions.

FRENCH HORS D'OEUVRES

Radishes: Scoop out a little of the radish and fill with butter.

Anchovies: Open cans and place in ravier. Leave in the tin.

Celery Root: Peel and cut celery root julienne-style. Cook until fork-tender. Cool and dress with mustard mayonnaise, made by adding Dijon mustard to mayonnaise.

Tomatoes: Peel and slice tomatoes. Place in even rows. Sprinkle with basil and dress with Russian Dressing (p. 61).

Paté: Buy in cans and open. Set in dish with a spreader and Melba toast.

Eggs: Hard cook eggs and cut in half lengthwise. Place well-flavored mayonnaise (mustard, white pepper, and chopped parsley) in ravier and set eggs on top, round side down.

Pickled Beets: Pickle beets (p. 74). Drain and dry on paper towel. Arrange in patterns. Garnish with chopped green onion.

ANTIPASTO

These are Italian hors d'oeuvres. They may be served in individual dishes such as raviers, but are more often attractively arranged on a large platter. They are served with either bread sticks called grissinni or with crusty Italian bread. They are hearty enough to make a complete lunch or supper with only the addition of a cup of soup and a hearty dessert.

Pickled Mushrooms: 1 pint of small fresh mushrooms, 2 tablespoons lemon juice, 1 tablespoon chopped onion, 3 tablespoons olive oil, ¼ teaspoon salt, a pinch of thyme. Cook 5 minutes. Chill mushrooms in the juice.

Fennel Vinaigrette: Wash and cut fennel in two lengths. Cook until fork- tender and marinate in Sauce Vinaigrette (p. 61).

Celery: Cut celery in two lengths and cook with 1 teaspoon fennel seed. Marinate in Sauce Vinaigrette (p. 61).

Zucchini: Scrub zucchini very well and slice medium thin. Arrange in rows and dress with Russian Dressing (p. 61).

Tuna: Open a can of albacore tuna and pour off oil. Marinate in Sauce Vinaigrette (p. 61), leaving in can. Place on platter whole and garnish as desired.

Cucumbers: Peel cucumbers but leave a little peel on. Score with fork. Slice medium thin and line up in ravier. Dress with Sour Cream Dressing (p. 62).

Potato Salad: Make from recipe (p. 84), and place in ravier.

Salami: Make little rolls from thin slices of salami. Secure with wood pick and place in ravier.

Bean Salad: Cook whole green beans. Marinate in Sauce Vinaigrette (p. 61). Chill and cover with Russian Dressing (p. 61).

Carrots: Cut carrots julienne-style. Cook until fork-tender. Marinate in Sauce Vinaigrette (p. 61).

Cauliflower: Cook flowerets until fork-tender. Marinate in Sauce Vinaigrette (p. 61).

Artichokes: Cook artichoke hearts until fork-tender. Marinate overnight in Sauce Vinaigrette (p. 61).

MEZZAS

Mezzas are popular appetizers of the Middle East, and they are often served as a complete meal in themselves. Accompanied by crisp Arabic bread, they are hard to beat.

Taramasalata: Soak 5 slices of white bread with crusts removed in 1 cup cold water for 5 minutes. Squeeze dry with hands. Place in blender and blend. Add juice of 1 lemon, 1 jar of red caviar or ½ cupTarama (Greek caviar), and a small onion. Blend 1 minute. Add ½ to ¾ cup olive oil, a little at a time, and blend between each addition. Serve in a lettuce-lined bowl and garnish with Greek olives. Serve with very crisp, warm Greek bread.

Garbanzos: Drain 1 (16 oz.) can garbanzos (chick-peas). Add ¼ cup chopped parsley, ¼ cup chopped onion, ½ teaspoon pressed garlic, 3 tablespoons lemon juice, 2 tablespoons olive oil, ½ teaspoon salt, and a pinch of cayenne. Mix well to coat each chickpea. Serve at room temperature.

Eggplant Purée: Wrap a medium-sized eggplant in foil and bake until tender. Cool slightly and peel. Chop and then mash, adding ¼ cup lemon juice, 1 large garlic clove (pressed), 1 teaspoon salt, 1 tablespoon olive oil, ¼ cup chopped onion, and 1 tablespoon chopped parsley. Taste for seasoning. Garnish with pine nuts, chopped parsley, and onion. Spread on crusty Arabic bread.

Tabbouleh: Place ½ cup burghul (fine cracked Greek wheat) in a bowl. Cover with cold water. Soak 10 minutes and drain in sieve lined with cheesecloth. Squeeze dry. Drop in bowl and add 3 tomatoes, 1 cup parsley, and 1 cup onions, all finely chopped. Add ¼ cup lemon juice, 2 teaspoons salt, ⅓ cup olive oil, and 1 tablespoon chopped mint. Serve on small leaves of Romaine lettuce.

Feta Cheese: This is a cheese that is kept in salt water brine. To serve, dry on towel and cut in cubes. Serve with bread or crackers.

SALAD ENSEMBLES

ANTIPASTO SALAD

1 (16 oz.) can kidney beans	1 cucumber, chopped
8 cooked carrots	10 radishes, chopped
½ pound fresh green beans, cooked	2 raw zucchini, sliced
Sauce Vinaigrette (p. 61)	3 tomatoes, cut in wedges
1 head Romaine lettuce, torn	10 ripe olives
1 head Boston lettuce, torn	1 (2 oz.) can anchovies
3 hard-cooked eggs, sliced	

Marinate kidney beans, carrots, and green beans in Sauce Vinaigrette. Toss assorted greens with Sauce Vinaigrette and place in salad bowl. Arrange all other ingredients in groups on top of lettuce. Serve with bread sticks or Italian bread. Makes 8 servings.

TOMATO AND CUCUMBER SALAD

Boston lettuce	2 slender cucumbers, sliced
3 small ripe tomatoes, sliced	Avocado Cream Dressing (below)

Line salad platter with lettuce leaves. Alternate slices of tomato and cucumber. Chill. Serve with Avocado Cream Dressing.

AVOCADO CREAM DRESSING

1 avocado	1 cup dairy sour cream
2 tablespoons lemon juice	½ teaspoon salt
½ teaspoon ginger	

Peel and cube avocado. Place all ingredients in blender and blend until smooth and creamy.

BUSY DAY SALAD

1 bunch carrots	Basic French Dressing (p. 61)
1 head cauliflower	Salad greens
1 bunch broccoli	2 hard-cooked eggs, chopped

Sauce Vinaigrette (p. 61)

Cook carrots, cauliflower, and broccoli separately. Do not overcook. Marinate in French dressing overnight. Wash and tear greens and store in plastic bag. Chop egg whites, sieve yolks and store in plastic bag. Just before serving, line salad platter with lettuce and add vegetables. Pour on Sauce Vinaigrette and sprinkle with egg garnish. This salad can be made the night before a busy day. Makes 6 servings.

MEXICAN SALAD

1 cup ripe olives, pitted	¾ cup mayonnaise
1 pound cooked shrimp	¾ teaspoon chili powder
1½ cups celery, sliced	1 head lettuce
3 tablespoons onion, chopped	2 tomatoes, sliced

Crisp corn chips

Cut olives in wedges. Mix with shrimp, celery, and onion. Mix mayonnaise with chili powder and stir into shrimp mixture, reserving some for extra dressing. Line platter with shredded lettuce. Arrange slices of tomato on lettuce. Mound shrimp on tomato slices. Arrange corn chips around base of salad and garnish with whole olives. Pass reserved dressing and corn chips. Makes 6 servings.

ACCOMPANIMENTS FOR SALADS

ROLLED SANDWICHES

1 (3 oz.) package cream cheese   3 tablespoons soft butter
3 tablespoons mayonnaise   Sandwich bread, thinly sliced
Small lettuce leaves

Mix cheese, mayonnaise, and butter well. Remove crust from bread and roll slightly with rolling pin. Spread with cheese mixture. Place a small lettuce leaf on bread, allowing lettuce to extend over the edges. Roll and place in cake pan. Cover with foil and refrigerate until ready to serve. These are attractive when served standing up in gravy boats.

POPPY SEED STICKS

Unsliced bread   ¼ pound butter
Poppy seeds

Cut unsliced bread in thin 1 inch slices. Remove crusts. Melt butter and have poppy seeds handy in saucer. Using a pastry brush, paint bread lightly with butter and dip lightly in poppy seeds. Place on cookie sheets and bake until brown. May be served either warm or cold.

CHEESE MACAROONS

1 (8 oz.) Jar Old English cheese   ¼ teaspoon salt
⅓ cup soft butter   Dash cayenne pepper
¾ cup flour   1 teaspoon paprika

Cream cheese and butter together well. Add dry ingredients. Press through a pastry tube in 1½-inch stars. Toast at 350° on greased cookie sheets until slightly brown. Sprinkle with paprika immediately upon removal from oven, and taste to make sure they are done.

TOASTED ENGLISH MUFFINS

English muffins   **Parsley, chopped**
Soft butter   **Green onions or chives, chopped**
                  Tarragon or basil, chopped

Split muffins and make an herb butter from the remaining ingredients. Toast muffins on cut side only and quickly spread with herb butter. Serve while hot.

Verna Meyer, a truly dedicated gourmet, has the reputation of knowing every herb, spice, fruit, vegetable, cheese, and wine that goes into the preparation of fine foods. Her cooking classes have aided hundreds of women in making delicious food for their families and guests.

She has attended Cordon Bleu in Paris, is a member of Les Societe des Gourmettes, and serves as Conseilliere Extraordinaire of the Minneapolis chapter of the Wine and Food Society. She conducts tours of Europe for "food and fun", and has had her own television show entitled "Way With Food."

Bon Appetit!

INDEX

SOUPS

Aioli Sauce, 40
Avocado Soup, Blender, 45
Avocado Soup, Caribbean, 47
Avocado, Cream of, 18

Bean Soup, Mexican, 29
Bean Soup, Navy, 27
Bean Soup, United States Senate, 30
Béchamel, Sauce, 13
Beet Soup, 41
Bisque, Crab, 40
Blender Avocado Soup, 45
Bombay Soup, 46
Borscht, 23
Bouillabaisse, American-Style, 38
Bouillabaisse, Easy, 47
Bouillon, 12
Bouillon, Court, 40
Bourride, 39
Broccoli, Cream of, 17
Broth, Quick and Easy, 11
Brown Stock, 11

Cantaloupe Soup, Cold, 44
Caribbean Avocado Soup, 47
Carrot, Potage of, 35
Cauliflower, Cream of, 19
Celery, Cream of, 20
Cheese Soup, 49
Chicken Noodle Soup, 26
Chinese Egg Flower Soup, 49
Chowder, Corn, 31
Chowder, Lima Bean and Mushroom, 34
Chowder, Manhattan-Style Clam, 37
Chowder, New England Clam, 36
Cioppino, 38
Cold Cantaloupe Soup, 44
Cold Senegalese, 43
Consommé, 12
Consommé Argenteuil, 14
Consommé Bouquetier, 14
Consommé Brunoise, 14
Consommé, Leek and Celeriac, 16

Consommé Moderne, 15
Consommé, Onion and Tomato, 16
Consommé Royale, 15
Corn Chowder, 31
Court Bouillon, 40
Crab Bisque, 40
Cream Clarmart, 46
Cream of Avocado, 18
Cream of Broccoli, 17
Cream of Cauliflower, 19
Cream of Celery, 20
Cream of Chicken Stock, 13
Cream of Cucumber Soup, 41
Cream of Lettuce, 18
Cream of Mushroom, 19
Cream of Shrimp Soup, 37
Cream of Tomato Neopolitan, 36
Cream of Tomato Portuguese, 36
Cream of Tomato Soup, 32
Cream of Vegetable, 17
Cream of Watercress, 18
Cucumber Soup, Cream of, 41

Dutch Pea Soup, 27

Easy Bouillabaisse, 47
Egg and Lemon Soup, 49
Egg Flower Soup, Chinese, 49
Essence of Mushroom Soup, 32

Farmer's Soup, 24
Fish Stock. See Quick and Easy Broth, 11
French Cream of Potato and Onion, 19
French Onion Soup, 21
Fruit Soup, 44

Game Soup, 30
Garbanzo (Chick-Pea) Soup, 30
Gazpacho, 43
Goulash Soup, 24
Gumbo Filé with Shrimp, 23

Ham and Celery Cabbage Soup, 29
Ham Stock, 12

Jellied Madrilene, 43

Lamb and Vegetable Soup, 22
Leek and Celeriac Consomme, 16
Lentil Soup, 28
Lettuce, Cream of, 18
Lima Bean and Mushroom Chowder, 34

Madrilene, Jellied, 43
Manhattan-Style Clam Chowder, 37
Mexican Bean Soup, 29
Mimosa Garnish, 33
Minestrone, 21
Mulligatawny, 28
Mushroom, Cream of, 19
Mushroom Soup, Essence of, 32

Navy Bean Soup, 27
New England Clam Chowder, 36
New-Fashioned New England
    Vegetable Soup, 22
Noodle Soup, Chicken, 26

Onion and Tomato Consommé, 16
Onion Soup, French, 21
Oxtail Soup, 25
Oyster Stew, 36

Pea Soup, Dutch, 27
Potage Aurore, 32
Potage Florentine, 33
Potage Monday, 32
Potage of Carrot, 35
Potage of Pumpkin, 33
Potage Red Mountain, 34
Potage St. Germain, 31
Potage Tomato, 35
Potato Almond Soup, 47
Pot-au-Feu, 25
Pumpkin, Potage of, 33

Quick and Easy Broth, 11

Royale, 15
Royale, Consommé, 15

Sauce Bechamel, 13
Savoy Cabbage Soup, 51
Senegalese, Cold, 43
Shrimp Soup, Cream of, 37
Smörgasbord Soup, 48
Soup Flamand, 50
Soup with a Flair, 50
Stew, Oyster, 36
Stock, Brown, 11
Stock, Cream of Chicken, 13
Stock, Ham, 12
Stock, Vegetable, 11
Stock, White, 12

Tomato Neopolitan, Cream of, 36
Tomato Portuguese, Cream of, 36
Tomato, Potage, 35

Tomato Soup, Cream of, 32
Turnip and Potato Soup, 28

United States Senate Bean Soup, 30

Vegetable, Cream of, 17
Vegetable Soup, New-Fashioned New
    England, 22
Vegetable Stock, 11
Vichyssoise, 42

Watercress, Cream of, 18
White Stock, 12

Accompaniments to Soup

Corn Bread, 53
Croustades, 54
Curry Rolls, 53
Garlic Croutons, 54
Homemade Noodles, 52
Meat Filling, 52
Parmesan Chips, 53
Pirozhki, 52
Pulled Bread, 54
Rye Bread Sandwiches, 52

SALADS

Antipasto, 86-87
Antipasto Salad, 89
Appetizer Salad, 79
Asparagus Vinaigrette, 72
Avocado Magnifique, 72

Bean Salad, Green, 75
Beet Salad, Pickled, 74
Beets, Pickled, 74
Big Salad, 83
Busy Day Salad, 90

Caesar Salad, 64
Cauliflower Salad, 71
Cherry Tomato Salad, 73
Chicken Salad, 80
Chiffonade Salad, 64
Chilled Tomato Salad, 73
Coleslaw, 67

Coleslaw, Creamy, 67
Crab Louis, 65
Crab Mousse, 81
Cream Slaw, Shrimp and Avocado on, 68
Creamy Coleslaw, 67
Cucumber Mousse, 65
Cucumber Salad, 64

Dinner Salad, 74

Eden's Salad, 77
Eggplant Salad, 76
Endive and Mushroom Salad, Fresh, 63

French Hors-d'Oeuvres, 86
Fresh Endive and Mushroom Salad, 63
Fresh Pineapple Salad, 79

Garden Salad, 74
Gourmet Spinach Salad, 69
Gourmet's Choice, 63
Greek Salad, 81
Green Bean Salad, 75
Green Goddess Salad, 82
Guacamole Salad, 71

Hors-d'Oeuvres, French, 86
Hot Potato Salad, 84
Hot Spinach Lettuce Bowl, 70

Imperial Salad, 83

Lebanese Salad, 85
Lettuce Salad, Wilted, 63

Mexican Salad, 90
Mezzas, 88
Mousse, Crab, 81
Mousse, Cucumber, 65

Peaches, Spiced, 78
Pickled Beet Salad, 74
Pickled Beets, 74
Pineapple and Avocado Salad, 77
Pineapple Salad, Fresh, 79
Potato Salad, Hot, 84
Potato Salad with Garnish, 84

Russian Salad, 80

Salad Bouquet, 68
Salad Cheval Bleu, 83
Salad Emeline, 85
Salad Louis, 75
Salad Nicoise, 82
Sauerkraut Salad, 70
Seafood Salad, 66
Shrimp and Avocado on Cream Slaw, 68
Spiced Peaches, 78

Spinach and Cucumber Salad, 69
Spinach Lettuce Bowl, Hot, 70
Spinach Salad, Gourmet, 69
Spinach Salad with Watercress Dressing, 70
Springtime Salad, 66
Summer Salad, 78
Sunburst Salad, 77
Surprise Salad, 78

Tomato and Cucumber Salad, 89
Tomato Salad, 73
Tomato Salad, Cherry, 73
Tomato Salad, Chilled, 73

Wilted Lettuce Salad, 63

Salad Dressings

Avocado Cream Dressing, 89
Bacon Dressing, 62
Basic French Dressing, 61
Basic Mayonnaise, 62
Celery Seed Dressing, 62
Chutney Dressing, 81
Classic Herb Dressing, 82
Dressing Magnifique, 72
Emeline Dressing, 85
French Dressing, Basic, 61
French Dressing, Honey, 78
Gloucester Sauce, 81
Herb Dressing, Classic, 82
Honey French Dressing, 78
Mayonnaise, Basic, 62
Mayonnaise Verte, 66
Olive-Caper Dressing, 71
Russian Dressing, 61
Sauce Louis, 65
Sauce Vinaigrette, 61
Sour Cream Dressing, 62
Sweet-Sour Dressing, 67
Tangy Dressing, 68
Tomato-Herb Dressing, 69

Accompaniments for Salads

Cheese Macaroons, 91
Poppy Seed Sticks, 91
Rolled Sandwiches, 91
Toasted English Muffins, 92